T0289555

ADVANCE PRAISE

'This collection is full of candid, fierce and challenging stories ... there is an overarching sense of joy and confidence that comes from talking openly about sex. *Doing It* is a very readable collection brimming with intelligence and intimacy.' ***Books+Publishing*** ★★★★

'Honest and insightful, these real-life stories peel back the sheets on the intimate awakenings of some of Australia's most talented writers. I loved *Doing It* and you will too.' **Clementine Ford**

'*Doing It* is a celebration of female desire and multi-sexualities in a world where women's bodies have come to be accepted as a mainstream icon for sex itself, while simultaneously and ironically denying that sex, and the libido, also exists in the female mind.' **Tara Moss**

Karen Pickering is a feminist organiser and writer based in Melbourne. She is the creator and host of Cherchez la Femme, a monthly talkshow of popular culture and current affairs from an unapologetically feminist angle, which has toured nationally. Karen was the cofounder of Girls On Film Festival and was its first director. She was also a founding organiser of SlutWalk Melbourne. She started doing it in 1992 and shows no signs of stopping.

DOING IT

WOMEN TELL THE TRUTH ABOUT GREAT SEX

EDITED BY
KAREN PICKERING

UQP

First published 2016 by University of Queensland Press
PO Box 6042, St Lucia, Queensland 4067 Australia

www.uqp.com.au
uqp@uqp.uq.edu.au

Cover design by Christabella Designs
Typeset in 12.5/18 pt Bembo Std by Post Pre-press Group, Brisbane
Printed in Australia by McPherson's Printing Group

Lyrics from 'Attraction Is Ephemeral' by Mecca Normal © Lester/Smith
SOCAN 2006. Reproduced with kind permission of Jean Smith.

National Library of Australia
Cataloguing-in-Publication data is available at http://catalogue.nla.gov.au

ISBN
978 0 7022 5423 9 (pbk)
978 0 7022 5823 7 (ePDF)
978 0 7022 5824 4 (ePub)
978 0 7022 5825 1 (Kindle)

University of Queensland Press uses papers that are natural, renewable
and recyclable products made from wood grown in sustainable forests.
The logging and manufacturing processes conform to the environmental
regulations of the country of origin.

CONTENTS

WE'RE ALL FEMINISTS, WE'RE ALL
WOMEN, WE'RE ALL SHARING INTIMATE
DETAILS OF OUR SEXUAL LIVES IN ORDER
TO MAKE A SPACE THAT TELLS OTHER
WOMEN, *YOUR BODY IS YOURS.*

INTRODUCTION

KAREN PICKERING

'Doing it' has always been one of my favourite ways of referring to sex. It's juvenile, of course, but also gleeful, conspiratorial, literal and cheeky. Making love, shagging, fucking, sleeping together, having sex, getting laid, banging – they're all fantastic and have their place, but somehow 'doing it' remains my preferred phrasing for this beloved pastime and undeniable fact of life. People have always done it, because if they hadn't we wouldn't be here, and if women didn't do it we'd have run out of humans a long time ago. So why do we have such a hard time accepting women as sexual creatures? What is it about a woman owning her sexuality that makes society so uncomfortable? How can we accept so much harm done to women because of this irrational fear that female sexuality is somehow dangerous? Some of the answers to these questions are very dark and scary and confronting indeed, but there's only one sure-fire cure for darkness and that's to fill it, flood it, with light.

So in this book we're going to talk about sex, read about it, think about it, and hear from incredibly different and equally compelling women on their positive experiences of sex. Why only positive recollections? I think there are good reasons to have spaces available to women for sharing their disastrous and disturbing sexual encounters, but I also believe strongly in the power of sharing our successes and reminding each other that there's a reason we keep going, keep engaging in this slightly bizarre ritual of smashing our bodies together for pleasure and joy and love – sometimes it is amazing, sometimes it changes us for the better, and, yes, sometimes it feels bloody good. Women don't get to talk about this, or hear it, enough.

It's always struck me as intensely odd that talking about sex can sometimes be harder than actually having it. That is, until you consider the reasons why our society makes it a tough topic to verbalise, especially for women. The social taboos around sex are inextricably linked to a fear of female sexuality and, no matter how you dice it, women are simultaneously expected to provide and facilitate sex (in specific and prescribed ways) while at the same time being 'appropriately' opposed to it. Be sexy but not too sexy. Love sex but only with me and not too much. Condemn other women for having too much sex lest you appear to be too into it yourself. Be sexually available but if you find yourself dealing with unintended consequences like pregnancy or infection or feelings of attachment then you're on your own. Perform your sexuality in acceptable ways but be ready at any moment to deny it, sublimate it or erase it entirely. This obviously impacts every person in our society, not least because of the immense pressure it places on women and the anxiety it causes that ripples out uncontrollably. It alienates us from our own bodies, makes us frightened of what we desire, and tells us that our sexual selves exist for others.

As a society we talk *about* women and sex a lot. You'll find a lot of panic buttons being hit over teenage girls being too sexually permissive, for instance. And the questions I can only answer with an eye-roll: Are women in offices dressing 'professionally' enough to be taken 'seriously'? Should older women 'put it away' and 'dress for their age'? Are women hurt by porn? Will they suffer less harassment if they change their clothes? Are they 'sexualising' themselves by sending nude selfies? All this discussion around us, angst projected onto us, policing of our collective sexuality, but we far less often ask women themselves about sex: how they do it, what they want from it, how it fits in with the rest of their rich and complicated lives. I thought it would be amazing to have a space for women to talk about sex in a positive light, without the usual pressures that tell them not to: needing to address the difference between bad sexual encounters and assault, apologising for their sexual desires, being backed into the corner of revealing just the right amount to titillate without compromising some imagined construction of integrity. Because any idea of integrity that requires you to excise whole parts of yourself in order to be respected is surely an abstract one, separate from the meaning of the word itself.

This pattern starts early. It's telling that most sex education offered to young people (often far too late) focuses on avoiding pregnancy and disease, and is delivered by adults who are embarrassed by the material. For girls there's an emphasis on reputation management and withholding themselves as the prize somebody will win for waiting the longest, being the nicest, exhibiting the most 'respect' and 'patience'. For boys there seems to be a tacit understanding that they're all sex-crazed automatons and that their responsibility begins and ends with keeping a condom in their wallet. And we can guess what same-sex attracted and gender-fluid kids make of all this – that they don't exist. That nobody actually helps kids to figure out what they want, what they like, and how they might navigate conversations to decide this together should provide us with clues as to why so many adults struggle with basic concepts like enthusiastic consent, pleasure, desire and mutual enjoyment. And this affects girls and women in specific ways that we can see played out over our adult lives, especially in our relationship with our sexuality.

The first time I had an orgasm I thought I might fly out the window. That's my solid memory – a fear? belief? that I would somehow slip through the security screen and end up outside in the yard, so out-of-body and unexpected was the experience. It was also thrilling and mind-numbing and definitely resulted in a short period of looking at my then-boyfriend as though he was some kind of god. It passed, and we broke up after he got angry when I vomited in his car at the end of a particularly big night out (he was blasting 'Rhythm Is a Dancer' at the time, so I maintain that it was not my fault). But as you might've guessed from this story, my first orgasm was not as early as it might've been. It was about four years after I became sexually active. And about a year before I started masturbating. That's some very weird maths.

Around the time of my first orgasm I read a book that changed my life (the original '70s version proclaimed that it would on the cover): *The Women's Room*, by Marilyn French. It's a classic of western feminism and while far from perfect remains a book that I press into the hands of anyone who hasn't read it and wants a glimpse into the radicalisation of many (white, middle-class) women into feminist ideas during the second wave. It's a book containing a lot of sex, much of it very bad; harrowing, even. It also vividly depicts sexual assault in ways that I'd never really encountered before – from the perspective of the survivors and without apology for the perpetrators. Towards the end, there's a particular sex scene for the protagonist, Mira, that set for me a powerful example of joyful, love-soaked, pleasure-drenched, romantic, organic, desperately hot sex. They fucked. I mean, really fucked. And afterwards they go to the fridge and pull out the makings of a salty feast that is then shared, devoured, on the bed – 'Jewish salami and feta cheese and hard-boiled eggs and tomatoes and black bread and sweet butter and half-sour pickles and big black Greek olives and raw Spanish onions and beer' – and to this day that's one of the sexiest things I can stand to think of. A lover I once had, who was terribly romantic and impossibly beautiful, made this exact meal for me once, knowing how much I adored the book and the scene, and I still cry when I think about that. Though it could also be because he later broke my heart.

So yes, sex is sometimes tied up with love, and longing and romance, but often it's not and I don't think the best sex I've had in life has been with the people I've loved the most. Some of it was with people I don't recall the names of. I've had incredible sex with people I actively dislike and sex I cringe to remember with people I've loved deeply and truly. There's the kind of sex you can't stop thinking about afterwards, where the electrical current still races through you and makes it hard to concentrate, sex in odd places (swimming pools, church pews, Greyhound buses, car bonnets, pub toilets), fast sex, slow sex, sex that's neither fast nor slow but goes on for hours, days even, in a haze of lust and half-sleep and occasional bursts of implausible energy. There's the sex you phone in and forget about even before it's over, the sex with the wrong person, or the wrong sex with the right person, or the kind of sex you think will be fantastic but in fact you regret forever and ever and ever amen. The sex that conceives children, under a blue moon, in a cold season, where the skin feels like heat itself and the world is about to change, has changed, utterly. There's sex with yourself, sometimes quick and perfunctory, other times slow and involved and almost luxuriating in the freedom of time and solitude, and then the sex that you imagine, alone or with others, where you can do things that you never would, or that aren't quite possible, or that work better as long as they stay in your head.

There are tiny moments in my sexual memory that I treasure for the oddest reasons. I remember a next-morning bonus fuck with a guy I'd brought home the night before, who was a bit older than me and impressively good in bed, and him telling me after that I had spectacular tits. I was so surprised because guys my age didn't tell you your body was great or how into it they were, and I was weirdly touched because it seemed such a spontaneous compliment and not from someone who was drunk. I think I blushed! And I've remembered it a million times since, especially when admiring my spectacular tits.

This collection is full of beautifully small observations and some bloody huge and profound ones. In the case of Hanne Blank's piece, it is both and much more besides. Recalling her story of one afternoon with a new lover, I can still feel the hairs on the back of my neck standing up straight, and myself in thrall to every detail and utterly transported by her words. Her vulnerability is truly her strength and this work is about the necessity of both – in our bodies, and in our connections with others.

Tilly Lawless takes us into her world(s) of bed as haven, bed as workplace, bed as site of explosive love, and you won't soon forget the electricity and honesty of her insights. Jenna Price shares her long love affair with sex, a gift from her implausibly randy parents, and one nurtured by the same relationship over decades of evolving desire and mutual trust. Michelle Law transports us back to adolescent bedrooms, and invites you to fill out a magazine sex quiz with a difference – she delivers far more knowing hilarity than I remember from any other sealed section.

Amy Gray explores the immediacy and intimacy of sexting, deftly situating it within a broader cultural analysis of sexual relationships that move between online and offline spaces in organic and powerful ways. Rosanna Beatrice talks sex and menses, pain and pleasure, illness and wellness and the bridges in between. Jane Gilmore reminds us that sexual selves aren't dependent on others, nor even do they require acting on every desirous impulse, and Brigitte Lewis interrogates the problem of heteronormativity in our shared understandings of female sexuality, and how much can be gained from queering that lens.

Clem Bastow goes back to where it all began – *Video Hits* – and guides us through her sexual awakening with sweetness and humility, concluding that initial ideas that sex should be fun and funny are worthy of lifelong consideration, while Maria Lewis reminds us that not every sexual encounter will be valuable for the reason we think it might be, and that learning from our mistakes is how we get better at putting ourselves first. Jax Jacki Brown tells her story of finding a home in her body, for her sexual spirit and political life, and the power she draws from accepting that the two are indivisibly linked.

Amy Middleton reflects on sex in strange places – abroad, atop buildings, in the imagination of men you meet in bars, in a relationship that is deemed less than legitimate in a society fixated on heterosexual coupling. Simona Castricum shares a deeply personal mapping of her sexual and psychological realities, linking them through an exegetic exploration of where they intersect, overlap and contradict. Adrienne Truscott gets playfully political, at the intersection of art, sex, travel, friendship, work and play, all with a bitchin' soundtrack of Prince, Barry White and Aerosmith.

Emily Maguire invokes Judas, prompting us to imagine just how many Australian girls (and boys) got their first pants feels from successive casts of *Jesus Christ Superstar*, and Deirdre Fidge talks performance pashing, Rubik's cubes and Melissa Etheridge with a sensitivity and lightness of touch that will make you want to squeeze her hand.

Van Badham opens up about sex and sobriety, as she walks the long road from alienation to connection through a series of life-changing decisions. Anne-Frances Watson shares her research on adolescent sexuality, and you might be surprised to find out what they don't know (and don't want to), while Sinead Stubbins revels in the heaving collective libido of millions of teenage girls, as she looks back at some of their all-time fave pop crushes, tracing a sexual awakening through music and community on phone screens, TVs and the pages of magazines.

Jessamy Gleeson surveys the feminist movement in the west and the power of sex positivity to liberate more than just our bodies. Giselle Au-Nhien Nguyen teases out the attraction between feminists and online dating by talking over the tough stuff with a bunch of cyberbabes, while Fiona Patten reflects on a life lived at the crossroads of politics and sex, in all their agony and, yes, ecstasy.

The words on these pages absolutely blew me away, every time I read them. When you assemble a collection like this, you dream of the kind of writing that warms, inspires, challenges, devastates and recalibrates. In the case of *Doing It*, we also had to share a political belief that women telling the truth about great sex has a lot do with power, and that we all live life through the prisms of both. We're all feminists, we're all women, we're all sharing intimate details of our sexual lives in order to make a space that tells other women, *your body is yours*. But the incredible diversity of our experiences should remind us all that however you do it is up to you, and the more we talk about that the more we'll challenge the narratives that hold women back from enjoying sex on their own terms. So go on, you know what to do.

IT'S TIME, LIKE PEACHES SAYS, TO RUB.

IN DESIRE OF LIP SERVICE: WOMEN WANT TO (FUCK) TOO

BRIGITTE LEWIS

Heterosexual women don't like sex. Lesbians die from bed death. Bisexuals just can't make up their minds. Women are naturally less desirous than men.

Bull (fucking) shit.

Turn your head to gaze at historical western representations of white, cis, heterosexual women, and you'll find the oft-recycled image of the passive woman and active man, which has been rolled out by sexologists since the eighteenth century. A heterosexual man is traditionally dominant, in control and full of desire (like an animal) in his sexual life, just like he's meant to be in the world. A woman is all that man is not: she is traditionally sexually submissive, plays at performing a 'catch me if you can' persona, and is only full of desire in response to male attention that magically and instantly turns her on (like an oven). Otherwise she's a dead fish, a starfish. Sigmund

Freud, one of psychology's superstars, famously told us the vagina has value only as a receptacle for the penis. Countless movies depict glazed-eyed women staring up at the ceiling as they wait patiently for the eager guy to pump himself to orgasm, almost as if pleasure were the domain of men and the clitoris were indeed a mythical entity not worth depicting, let alone touching.

The discourse or language around sexual desire and gender in western society is slower to change than a hypothetical lightbulb. But that's because it serves the purpose of maintaining power structures that dictate what male and female behaviour should be like, what men and women should do and like in bed, and who gets to speak about the norms of such behaviour. Transgender women's sexuality isn't even spoken about.

Social theorist Paula Nicolson calls this a knowledge cycle, in which already dominant ideas about women and sexuality get recycled while feminist critiques often become the stuff of media derision – if they are even reported. The popular imagining of the feminist as being a man-hating butch lesbian has worked wonders at persuading women and men that they are in fact not feminists and don't need it or want anything to do with it (not to mention the demonising of presenting or identifying as butch and/or lesbian).

Even the word 'vagina' is an extension of male sexuality; it's a Latin word for 'sheath'. So, not only have women been denied sexual agency or desire of their own by being labelled as sexually passive, but even vaginas are considered a covering for a penis. Sometimes they are, but the etymology sure as hell tells us who gets to write, name *and* problematise female sexuality.

In Ancient Egypt all female illnesses were related to what they thought was a wandering womb – in other words, if a woman was sick it was because she was a woman and not a man. Even a sore throat was diagnosed as a purely female sickness, and its cure was seminal discharge. Later, the Greeks advised in their own 'seminal' texts that a wandering womb was a result of inadequate sexual relations and cured by marriage. Then came Christianity. In the creation story known as 'The Fall' Eve is blamed for the corruption of the entire human race because of her uncontrollable desire. A few hundred years later in the latter half of the fifteenth century, the witch trials erupted, persecuting largely single, widowed, lower-class women who were deemed dangerous and wild because they had no man to control their sexuality, their carnal lust, the devil inside. Society beware!

The Victorian era swept in and signalled a new theory of hysteria, brought about by what was called excess sexuality. It was, unlike male hysteria, not cured by masturbation, but by sex with a husband and, later, male doctors stimulating women to hysterical paroxysm (now known as the female orgasm). The vibrator was actually invented by these same doctors with tired fingers so they could deliver themselves from the tiresome task of finger-banging them all. William Acton, a sexuality expert of the era said that 'the majority of women (happily for them) are not very much troubled by sexual feeling of any kind', which goes a long way to telling you why they thought female orgasm was hysterical paroxysm and not in fact actual female orgasm.

Female hysteria was also convenient. What brings heterosexual men to orgasm the quickest? A vagina. But rather than contemplate what women needed to orgasm, it was easier for men to stigmatise women's sexuality and turn it into a disease. Any woman across any age could be diagnosed with hysteria. If she was sensitive, intelligent, sexual, liked to masturbate – basically, if she was an actual real-life desiring woman – it was off to the doctor's with her and then home for bed rest and little else, doctor's orders. In 1905, Freud believed that women's sexuality was 'a dark continent', irrational and unknowable, but still announced that 'only immature women have clitoral orgasms and real women, mature women, have vaginal orgasms'. Unsurprisingly, the rate of women faking orgasm increased.

Now fix your gaze on current depictions of women and you'll find that the narrative remains disturbingly similar, at least in western popular culture. Women are in the double bind of being expected to be sexually available, but not *too* sexually available. Their number of sexual partners can never run into double digits, let alone triple.

If a woman projects a sexual image of too much confidence, if she speaks about her desire, her sexual history, she is still liable to be called a 'slut', 'easy', a 'whore', a 'fucking cunt'. Cunt, after all the feminist movement's attempts to change the meaning of the word, is still the worst thing anyone can be called. Simultaneously though, female desire is considered to be less powerful than men's.

Heterosexual and bisexual women experience much higher rates of sexual dissatisfaction across their lives. Exactly why this is so remains the subject of taboo and very little research. What women think and feel about sex and their own desire is woefully absent from the conversations about them. What we do know is clitoral stimulation is how most women orgasm, yet revulsion of the cunt persists, and reciprocity when it comes to fellatio and cunnilingus remains unequal. We do have stats to work with – a 2006 Australian study by Juliet Richters found that 60.9 per cent of heterosexual women had an orgasm in their last sexual encounter compared to 94.8 per cent of heterosexual men. Only 50 per cent of these women achieved orgasm through penetrative sexual intercourse.[1] Part of the problem then is how we conceptualise 'real sex' and a woman's role in it. Many women are reluctant to talk about what they need to come because more often than not it's more than a simple in-and-out action, a fact that challenges everything many of us have been taught about sex, orgasm and desire. It asks us to refocus our collective attention away from the vaginal opening and what it does for and to men, and onto the clitoris and what it can and does do for many women. It's time, like Peaches says, to rub.

Most interestingly, recent research by sexologist Meredith Chivers, popularised by Daniel Bergner (yes, another white man writing about female sexuality) in his 2013 book *What Do Women Want?*, found that while women self-report feeling less desire to a variety of stimuli compared to men, their instantaneous bodily responses say otherwise. In 2007 Chivers and Amanda Timmers conducted a Canadian experiment with women and men, heterosexual and homosexual, to gauge both their subjective self-reported responses and clinically tested reports of arousal in response to a series of sexual video clips. These included a man sliding himself inside a woman on a green army blanket, a beautiful muscular man walking along the beach with a limp dick, a woman licking another woman's clit in the bath, a man sucking another man's large cock, a naked woman performing callisthenic leg scissoring and two bonobos mating. They found that heterosexual women were only reporting their heterosexual desire, but their bodies reported desire for each of the scenarios. Heterosexual men, on the other hand, knew exactly when they were and when they weren't aroused, and they weren't at all aroused by bonobos fucking, unlike the hetero and lesbian women. In other words, heterosexual men reported levels of desire in alignment with their sexual identity, while heterosexual women's desire was gender non-specific, even if they stated otherwise – they were aroused by men and women despite identifying as heterosexual.[2]

What I think this gestures at is that women are allowed to be sexual objects, and perform sexual desire, but the cultural rules around what women are allowed to feel permeates our realities so deeply that we sometimes cut ourselves off from our bodies, or at least from talking about what our bodies are feeling. It's ironic because women have historically been associated with the body and men the mind. But women have had to embody a very particular idea of 'the body'. A good heterosexual woman desires only her husband, is empathetic, caring and sensitive, but represses all other desires in pursuit of the eternal feminine. She becomes the enduring image of the soft, virgin-like woman who wants nothing more than to carry children, cook and, if she's lucky, work part-time and occasionally fuck her sexually deprived husband on his birthday. Chivers and Timmers's research highlights how much women are coerced into silence about what they feel.

Anthropologist Michael Herzfeld talks about the cultural secrets carried by people from the same nation. (For instance, by virtue of being Australian, you're meant to buy into the idea that everyone gets a fair go even though we have an increasing gender pay gap.) Women have, I reckon, particular kinds of cultural secrets. Some of us quite literally pay lip service to our desire. Women want to fuck (a lot) too. So while heterosexual women may not self-report feeling a high level of desire for other women fucking, bonobos fucking, men fucking each other, a man walking along the beach with a limp dick, or a woman touching herself, it doesn't mean they don't feel that desire, it just means they're not talking about it. The ideal heterosexual woman doesn't feel aroused when she sees sex between apes, women or gay men (how embarrassing). Except maybe she does? Every single woman in Chivers and Timmers's study did, regardless of her sexuality. This is what I'm calling a closed-mouthed, open-lipped secret. More recent research in 2015 replicating Chivers and Timmers's original study found that heterosexual women were now self-reporting gender non-specific desire and it was being captured in their bodily measurements. Cultural evolution is happening, even if the research is largely cisnormative and heterocentric.[3]

Another study by Chivers and Timmers from 2012 debunked the long-held and culturally perpetuated belief that what women want is emotional intimacy. The participants in this study maintained that they were least aroused when hearing audio stories about attractive male strangers – yet their genital blood throbbed more intensely than what they reported. Add to this that the story about the broad-chested male friend produced an almost flat-lined vaginal pulse, and the idea that women want and respond only to security and safety was seriously challenged.[4]

Representations of women as socially desire-less or pathologically desire-full are an important reminder of how far we have to go in understanding, valuing and investing in women's sexual stories, in women's voices.

Some women, I am told, said no to the opportunity to contribute to this collection because they thought talking about their own desire and sexual experience could hurt their careers or reputations. When this thought becomes the stuff of historical eye-rolling, then we will have made progress.

Back in 1975 Australian historian Anne Summers, in her book *Damned Whores and God's Police*, called our attention to the fact that women were still only really allowed to occupy the role of the virgin (God's police) or the slut (the damned whore). Sluts are women out of order who threaten the patriarchal arrangement of sexual men and passive women. Sadly, nearly forty years later slut-shaming is still a thing – but so is SlutWalk.

Today we hear about fuckboys on Tinder and women being taken advantage of by men who just want them for their own pleasure. But we hear little of what women on Tinder want or experience, which may be, like their male counterparts, to fuck. When did you last hear a real-life woman even speaking the words *I like to fuck*? Shame about our own desire is embedded in us from the day we're born; fear of being labelled less feminine, a gender outlaw, loose. Slut-shaming as we now know it serves an ideological function: to push a woman back into sexual passivity where history says she belongs, to keep her quiet about her desires, because it is the woman's sexual constraint and disciplined body that enables monogamy, hetero-sexual marriage, the nuclear family, the maintenance of traditional gender norms and the re-inscription of patriarchal power structures. Women can then either be good ideological subjects and bow to ideas about what their bodies should feel and do: moisturise – go to the gym – close your legs – be sexually adventurous – take charge but don't be bossy – remove your body hair – don't sleep with too many people. Or they can resist this kind of disciplining of their bodies and minds and reclaim their suppressed desire, one fuck-related word, one feeling, one swipe-right at a time.

IT WAS EXACTLY LIKE SAUL'S ROAD TO
DAMASCUS CONVERSION I'D LEARNT
ABOUT IN SUNDAY SCHOOL – EXCEPT THE
BRIGHT LIGHT WAS JUDAS'S CROTCH,
AND INSTEAD OF BEING STRUCK BLIND
I WAS STRUCK HORNY.

KISS ME, JUDAS

EMILY MAGUIRE

I don't remember the first time I watched the 1973 film *Jesus Christ Superstar*. It was one of many parentally approved VHS tapes in the cabinet next to the TV, the kind of thing my siblings and I would stick in the machine as background noise on weekend afternoons. I do, however, remember – vividly – the moment I realised I really, really wanted to fuck Judas Iscariot.

I was an intensely bookish, devoutly Christian twelve-year-old and I'd never said the F-word out loud. I'm pretty sure I'd never even thought it. I'd definitely never thought about it in terms of something I might want to do with someone else. But there I was, on an ordinary Saturday afternoon, reading a book while this old movie I'd half-seen twenty times played. I glanced up, saw, as if for the very first time, Our Lord's traitor (as played by Carl Anderson) in his hide-nothing, tasselled jumpsuit, and – boom – there it was. It was exactly like Saul's Road to Damascus conversion I'd learnt about in Sunday school – except the bright light was Judas's crotch, and instead of being struck blind I was struck horny.

As a good Christian girl I was troubled as much by the idea of wanting to do *that* at all as I was by the idea of wanting to have anything to do with the man who betrayed Jesus with his kiss. But, oh, the hours I spent imagining what that kiss must have felt like.

A year or so later at Bible camp I was in a one-on-one 'rap' session with a youth leader called Danni. The point of these sessions was to share the burden of our sins so we could then walk more lightly alongside Jesus. It began badly when I said I had a confession: Danni cut me off and proceeded to explain – at great length – how it absolutely was not a confession because confessing was what Catholics did and we were Protestants and here were all the ways in which we were different. But finally I was able to *share the burden* of my lustful thoughts.

Danni reassured me that having sexual thoughts was totally normal, but also, she said, I should try not to because before too long I wouldn't be satisfied with the thoughts alone and I might feel moved to act on them. I assured her I would never do that. I was pretty sure Carl Anderson didn't even live in Australia. 'I'm talking about sinning against your own body,' she told me. And I was so confused and shocked I didn't ask for any details, but that very night in my hard, narrow camp bed, while nine other girls sniffled and snored around me, I started to figure it out.

Danni must've suspected that our rap session hadn't done the trick of turning my mind towards purity, because a few weeks later as I was leaving Friday-night youth group she handed me a book. *Kari* was a yellowing paperback with a heavily creased spine. The fading cover showed a blond teenage girl posing sexily in a mini-skirt while stern-faced, sensibly dressed people glared at her from the side. The tagline was: *She needed love, but where could she find it?*

Kari was my introduction to John Benton's *Living Hope* series of Christian cautionary tales for wayward girls. Each had a single-name title, a cover picture of a girl looking hot in a '70s kind of way and a teasingly dark tagline. As I read my way through the travails of Kari, Cindy, Sherri, Nikki, Lori, Marji and the rest, I stopped thinking about Judas and his kiss and started fantasising about the seriously hot stuff that these girls (whose names all ended in an -ee sound — *like mine*) were getting up to. They weren't just kissing boys, they were getting knocked up and pimped out by them. They were running away from home and moving into apartments where lights flashed outside constantly and other sexy girls lay around and talked about all the men *they'd* been doing it with. They smoked and drank and injected things I'd never heard of, and wore really high heels and a lot of makeup and very tight clothes which drove men *out of their minds*. One of them robbed a chemist! Another ended up taking part in some wild

Satanic ritual! All of them had men pawing at them and begging them to *do it* with them all the damn time.

What happened in the last fifth of every book was that the girl was saved by a character called, not coincidentally, John Benton and taken to a kind of Christian detention centre for naughty girls, where the protagonist repented everything and was born again in the eyes of the Lord. After the first few I stopped reading as soon as the saving started. I got the message: live wild and repent later, girl. Jesus'll take you whenever.

Sadly, as a chubby, nerdy adolescent living in Sydney's Bible belt in the late 1980s, opportunities to embrace the lifestyle of Kari et al. were non-existent, and so all I could do was sin against myself while imagining the stuff the books left out – all the specifics of what happened between taking the good-looking older man's hand and crying brokenly in an inner-city drug den.

I thought my chance to sin with someone else might be approaching when it came time for the Years 7–8 Bible camp. We were teenagers! Away without our parents! Sleeping in buildings next to each other! And on the program was a session called 'The Truth about "Doing It"'. I felt like my whole life had been leading up to this moment. Finally, I'd get some details with which to flesh out my imaginings.

Yes, my expectations were a little over the top, but even so the session was objectively terrible. We were split up into boys' and girls' groups, and instead of being told anything at all about how to do it we got a lecture on how doing it would lead to:

a) pregnancy

b) warts and fungus on your bits at best, dying from AIDS at worst (probably all three, to be honest)

c) hatred from the boy you did it with because you led him away from the kingdom of heaven, thanks very much

d) the loathing of everyone in your community once they found out, and they *would* find out trust me everyone *knows* who's done it, they just do.

And even if you managed to somehow get away without any of the above (it might happen, don't know how, but let's just say), doing it would still lead to:

e) more suffering for Jesus because every time you sin it's like another nail being driven into his palms; and

f) the devastation of one day meeting your true love and not being able to offer him the ultimate gift of your virginity.

After all that heartfelt terrorising we were told to go back to our rooms and write a letter to our future husband, promising to wait for him and explaining why. I started with the best of intentions, mimicking the language of the group leader – sacred bond, ecstasy of a union blessed by God, blah blah blah – but as I thought about how much I wanted sex now and how it was years and years until I'd get married, I realised that my wedding night was going to be a truly epic sexplosion and my future true love should be warned. Writing about what that would be like, about exactly what he could expect, started to be really fun and really exciting and ...

And if I could barely make it to the gross concrete-and-steel campsite toilet in order to get myself off after merely writing down what I thought it would be like, then how the hell was I going to wait for years to actually do any of it? To hell with waiting (and with me, I supposed). I tore up the letter/amateur erotica and flushed it.

A few months later a boy from my church kissed me at a school dance. When he pulled away I tried to go in for more but he held up a hand. 'You're someone's future wife,' he said to me. 'I have to think: what if someone was doing this to my future wife? Like, do unto others, you know?'

Yeah, I knew. I was gagging to do unto others what I'd been doing to myself. Still, having actual knowledge of what a tongue in my mouth and hands on my waist felt like meant that the self-doing reached previously undreamt-of heights that night. As I was drifting off into a deeply satisfied sleep, I remembered a recent youth group session.

Our leader had ripped a piece of sticky tape off a cute Mickey Mouse dispenser. 'This is *great* tape,' she'd said with late-night infomercial enthusiasm. 'Suuuuper sticky.'

'But look!' She stuck it to her t-shirt, pulled it off. 'Uh-oh, less sticky now. And what if I do this—' She stuck it to the top of the girl sitting closest to her, then pulled it off again. 'And this!' Stick, unstick on another kid's shirt.

'And again!' She kept this up until she'd pressed the tape against us all.

'Ugh. Will you look at it now?' She paraded the piece of tape around, a sad, crinkled little sliver layered with fuzz of several different colours.

'Yuck, huh? But here's the thing, you guys! When you have sex with someone – yeah, I did it, I said the S-word! – when you do that with someone else, you don't come away clean. You come away with bits of them stuck to you and something essential about you has been lost forever. You end up like this tape.' She made a big deal of trying to get it to stick to the whiteboard behind her, then, with a tragic sigh, she scrunched it into a ball and dropped it in the bin.

Everybody nodded and acted disgusted and impressed, which was the standard way to react when this kind of demonstration took place (there'd been others: the Chupa Chup which no-one wanted to lick once the first kid had sucked on it; the collages of cardboard hands layered over a police-outline blob of a body until the body was covered; the story about a temple in which careless visitors stomp mud into the floor, break vases and smash windows and when the long-awaited prophet arrives he can't pray there because it's such a mess).

That night after my first kiss, though, I decided that, the way I felt now, going further would be totally worth the risk. After all, that tape was still usable after the first stick-unstick. If I could just have sex once – maybe not even go all the way, but, say, a bit of inside-the-undies action – once, maximum twice, before I was married, I thought it'd be alright.

When I finally met a boy willing to put his hands in my pants, however, I did feel pretty much the way I'd been warned I would. Not during – all I was feeling then was YES – but afterwards, I was smothered with regret and fear. All the stuff from Bible camp and Scripture and the girls-in-peril books flooded my mind. I hadn't done anything that could get me pregnant and I was pretty sure those smooth, clean boy hands couldn't have infected me with anything nasty, but I *could* feel the imprint of those hands on me hours and hours after they'd withdrawn. Shit! It was true. There was no clean ripping away that piece of tape! It – *I* – was marked forever.

And, you know, I wasn't sure of the boy's name (it was noisy and he mumbled) and I couldn't be sure I'd recognise him if I saw him again (it was dark and most of the time his face was smushed against mine) but I *did* feel profoundly connected to him. It felt horribly likely that on my wedding night I would be unable to help thinking of him, of the way I gave myself up to his fingers. It felt true that, as I'd been told, I could never go back – my temple had been trashed, and when the one I should have been waiting for entered, he would turn away in disgust.

But within a week, as the shock of having done something so forbidden wore off, I realised I felt okay. Pretty good, even. Actually, the only thing that'd been awful was those hours of lying in bed afterwards labelling the feeling I got when I remembered how his fingers felt inside me as 'being marked forever', recasting the sense of wholeness and connection I'd felt at orgasming in someone else's presence as a terrible thing that would ruin my future marriage, and visualising myself as a ruined temple when I was, in fact, a goddamn queen who'd just claimed ownership of her sparkling pleasure palace and could invite in whomever she pleased.

The disconnect between how I felt and what I'd been told I should feel didn't make me lose my faith in God (that happened later) but I did become a sceptic about youth leaders and ministers and Scripture teachers and bloody John Benton when it came to sex. The more sexually active I became, the more it was obvious that these people had no idea what they were talking about.

I don't want to over-romanticise this period of my life – I was a desperately horny teenager smashing up against other desperately horny teenagers, and things sometimes got messy and painful. But mostly, being sexual made me feel really fucking great about myself, and I knew that if I told any of the church people this, they would diagnose me as suffering from a tragic God-deficit. I would be Kari *looking for love in the beds of strangers when all she needed to do was look into her heart where God was waiting.*

But it wasn't about love or approval or lack of faith in myself or God. It was about finding a thing I was good at and enjoyed. It was about discovering that the value of my body was not in what it looked like to others but in how it could feel and help others feel.

I never felt used (though I did sometimes feel disrespected, which was unpleasant but a common experience in my life at the time anyway, since teenagers tend to be disrespected by the world at large simply for existing).

I never felt damaged or ruined (though I was occasionally hurt, because that's what happens sometimes when people get involved with other people, whether it's for an hour or a week or a lifetime, clothes on or off).

I never felt that my sexual choices would have a long-term impact on my life (and I was right, though I see now that a lot of that was down to luck since I'd had *no* proper sex-ed, goddamn it).

I did begin to feel hated and abused, though. Not by the guys I was hooking up with but by my religious leaders. Listening to the untruths and ignorance about what was, for me, an important and overwhelmingly positive part of growing up and finding out who I was in the world made me feel like an absolute piece of crap.

So I stopped going to church and youth group and school Scripture. I kept having sex. And, look, it's only been a couple of decades so I can't say for sure but, given that I haven't yet robbed a chemist shop or taken part in any Satanic rituals, I think I can say it's all going to be alright.

I DID NOT HAVE TO WONDER HOW IT
LOOKED OR HOW IT SOUNDED OR WHAT
HE MIGHT THINK, BECAUSE I KNEW
WHAT HE THOUGHT AND WHAT HE
THOUGHT WAS THAT HE WANTED ME.

ROOM 408

HANNE BLANK

It had been years since I'd felt wanted, felt desired, felt like someone was holding their breath in anticipation of me. Naturally I'd tried to tell myself that this was normal, predictable; that the thing about five years, ten years, thirteen years of a relationship is that lust never hangs around the scene of a crime too long and, anyway, isn't there more to life?

I'd always wanted more sex than my partner, even at the beginning. I told myself that this, too, was normal, predictable; that sometimes this happens, that choosing your person means sometimes making choices about what you can live with, as well as about the things you are happy to embrace. I could live with a difference in libido. After all, it was only sex and, anyway, I owned a vibrator and had two fully functional hands.

Somewhere around year six I decided I was tired of

initiating sex, so I quit in protest. It was also an experiment. I made no declaration, drew no line in the sand, said nothing. It would be, I figured, a chance for me to put my money where my mouth was about there being more to life, about what I could live with, about where my real priorities were in a relationship.

In any case, I could write about sex even if I wasn't having any. In the nine months it took before my partner finally decided to seek out sex with me, I wrote an entire book of erotica and sold it: a book of all the sex I wasn't having and would never have had with that particular partner anyway. Too much of it was too kinky, too intense, too much about my own particular likes and peculiarities and appetites to have flown in that relationship. Yet it's still selling copies from its little perch in my publisher's back catalogue. Once a year, I get a small royalty cheque. Who knew nine months without sex could pay dividends?

Hindsight, of course, is the clearest sight. I look back now and can't imagine quite how – for many reasons, not just the sex issue – I stayed in that relationship another nine years. Naturally it was nine years of every excuse, every rationalisation, every worry and sorrow and fear. Things tied us together. We travelled shared ruts. I was afraid of what might happen if I left. But, as they sometimes do, things got worse, and eventually I became afraid of what might happen if I stayed.

About a year before I left, I knew I had to go. I was scared and unsure, though, and by no means certain how one left a relationship that one had been propping up, holding together, shoving onwards through all manner of things, for so many years. When it has been your daily habit to hold on tight to something no matter what, peeling your fingers away and uncurling your clenched fist is hard.

Besides, it had been years since I'd felt sexy, felt desired, felt like someone's heart, or indeed any other portion of their anatomy, surged for the want of me. It was part of my pain and part of my fear. We measure the size of relationships in months, in years, and with each anniversary the relationship grows larger, thicker, heavier. It can block out the sun. After a while, it becomes difficult to imagine that anyone could react to you differently than your partner does; that anyone could treat you differently, think of you differently; that anyone ever had. If I could expect nothing different, I wondered, would it actually be worth the trouble and pain of leaving? If no-one else would want me, should I perhaps stay where at least I knew the nature of the bargain, however disappointing and sad?

Then I went to another city in another state to a conference to give a paper. While I was there I went out to supper with a long-time online friend I'd never met in person. While we were at supper, I realised I was on a date.

A first date. A really, really good first date. A crackling and sexy and delicious and soulful first date, the kind where you annoy the wait staff at the restaurant by dawdling and laughing and ordering another drink so you can nurse it forever because as long as you're still working on your drink you can still be talking. The kind where you don't actually leave the table until well after the waiter has begun to give you side-eye. When we finally did leave the restaurant my body was a high-voltage wire, currents of mutual interest and desire rushing hard and fast. I was high on it, drunk on it, dazzled and lightheaded with it. I couldn't remember having ever wanted a kiss as badly as I did as we walked back to the car, as I looked up at a cold bone-white moon and tried not to hold my breath.

I did not get kissed that night. The next day I was headed back home, to my sexless bed and a withering gut-punch of derision, suspicion and guilt-trip that I had gone away and – gasp! – had a good time, that I had come home strangely happy, full of mischief and the deep joy of having been seen and heard and wanted. It was not much longer before I announced that it was over, that I was leaving.

I want this much to be clear: I did not leave my partner of fifteen years for someone I had never so much as kissed. I left my partner of fifteen years because it was time to leave, because things were broken beyond repair, because there comes a point where they're not worth fixing. I left my partner of fifteen years because my partner had never in fifteen years left me breathless with the force of our mutual longing for nothing more than a kiss. And though I did end up kissing the friend I'd gone out with that November night, I didn't do it until after I announced that I was done, that the partnership was finished, that as soon as we could tidy up loose ends, I would be leaving.

We kissed, it turned out, thanks to another conference, one that brought my friend close to where I lived. He wrote to ask if I'd be able to see him while he was in the area. Would I come visit for the afternoon? When I said yes, he asked a favour. When I asked what sort of favour, he said, 'I just want five minutes with you, in private, so I can kiss you.'

Every cliché is true once, I believe, and quite a few were true in those five minutes. The world disappeared. My knees turned to jelly. My heart pounded so hard I was sure other people could hear it. My sense of time passing decided it had better things to do than watch two middle-aged people kiss, and wandered off to the conference hotel bar for a beer. Eventually my friend and I figured maybe passers-by, too, had better things to do than watch two middle-aged people kiss, and shyly, a little primly, we giggled our way up to his room.

Where we did not, for the record, fuck.

No, it was better than that. For the next several hours, what we did was wallow in our wanting. We kissed and touched and groaned and whispered, nibbled and caressed and gasped. I let my head fall back and my eyes close and simply savoured it when he kissed my neck, my collarbones, my breastbone, when he nuzzled down into the neckline of my blouse and the cleavage below. At one point I turned around to dig something out of my purse, and he noticed that my stockings, plain beige nylons by

DOING IT

all front-looking appearances, were seamed. He fell to his knees and worshipped them, and my legs beneath them, with fingers and lips and exclamations of delight and wonder.

Our voices grew hoarse with arousal. My panties were soaked and my nipples so hard they could've cut glass. I was dizzy with desire, with being desired, with the thickness and the sweetness of the want and the friction between us. That afternoon, behind the closed door of Room 408, the *do not disturb* sign hung on the doorknob, was so many things I had ached for over such a very long time. It was so many things I had told myself didn't matter for so many years that I'd long since stopped wishing for them, and so many things I thought someone like me would simply never have. It was things I'd forgotten existed, or perhaps never knew did. It was lust, pure but not simple, and also something deeper, something more serious than 'lust' implies. It was the connected yearning of two people in early middle age who were both scarred and scared, and more than half convinced that no-one would want them again, and who thought they were probably stuck with it, but whatever, they would just have to learn to live with it.

Until they didn't.

There may be more glamorous kinds of magic in the world but there are few truer, and I came hard, that afternoon, from nothing more than the scrape of teeth on the side of my neck and the press of a palm cupping my breast. I came without preamble and without warning, a long

30

ecstatic shudder over the edge of a cliff whose edge I hadn't even seen. It delighted and shocked us both, we who had been friends for years but barely known one another long enough in person to pick each other out in a crowd if we'd had to.

It was so easy. I could simply stand there and be wanted, lean in for a kiss and let my body have its way. I did not have to wonder how it looked or how it sounded or what he might think, because I knew what he thought and what he thought was that he wanted me. The Rubicon of my underthings remained uncrossed, and that was easy too, because fucking was never the point. The point was that we wanted one another and that was enough.

When I came, the surprise in his eyes was real, as was the deep pleasure, and the gratitude. I blushed, red-eared and flustered, upended, suddenly unsure whether things had just gone too far, unsure what to make of the inexplicable gravity of our collision. After a long moment, he solved the problem by kissing me, touching me, wanting me until it happened again.

There is more to the story. There is always more to the story, with a story like this one, and it goes much as you might expect a story about longed-for things and broken things and urgent things and desperate things to go. There was no happily-ever-after for my friend and me, no wandering hand in hand into some glowing re-marital sunset. There was pain, in the end, as thick and as hot as the pleasure.

But that is not the point. The point is that fifteen years of partnership can lie, and sometimes does, and it can hide its lies in the long shadow that fifteen years casts. The point is that I was allowed to remember what I'd tried to forget, given not just a chance but a blessing to want things I never knew I had a chance at. The point is that for a few indelible moments I was so beautiful and so wanted and so stunned that I could do nothing but believe it, and know it, and feel it in my blood, and I can never forget it or cast it away. The point is that I am saying thank you.

WHEN YOU HAVE NEVER SEEN BODIES
LIKE YOURS BEING SEXUAL, THERE IS
POWER IN FINALLY SEEING IT, AND EVEN
MORE POWER IN FINDING IT FUCKING HOT!

FUCKABILITY: EXPLORING MY DISABILITY AND QUEER SEXUALITY

JAX JACKI BROWN

The first time I came, I thought I was dying. You know that rush: the out-of-body experience that is so very in your body at the same time. I lay on my back, with strategically placed pictures of Leonardo DiCaprio staring down at me from my pink-walled room with its lime-green trim – I had requested this; I was going to be a girl and like what other girls liked; I was going to fit in – and wondered what had just happened. I was twelve and in love with Anna Paquin, whose cut-out picture from *Dolly* was bravely tacked in among the boys close to my bed.

I should have known what an orgasm was. My family was very left-leaning and I had been given 'the sex talk' more than once. The talk mostly consisted of my mother telling me to 'never let a man into bed with you unless he has a condom on *at all times*'. There was never any mention of consent or same-sex attraction, or my disability. My different muscles, my impending wheelchair, were, at this time, a source of shame for me and the rest of my family.

Orgasms offered me an escape, a means of imagining myself into a different body, a body that did not have disability. Sex in my mind, with this new imagined body, was free from all the parts of myself that I was struggling with. Wanking became like a gateway drug – a gateway into the body I longed for, a way of entering a different world even if just for a moment, to almost be able to grasp this body in the transcendence of orgasm.

So I became a bit of a wanker. I'd have my hit first thing in the morning, in the day if I could sneak away and at night to help me sleep. I was in exile from my body but I was also being drawn into it by ecstasy, marvelling at its capacity for pure pleasure, finding elation in the magic of orgasms.

I should have known I was into women because of the way I felt around my friend at school – both aroused and terrified – and how I didn't feel anything for the boys she was crushing on and talking about obsessively. I should have known by the way she made me weak at the knees and glad to be sitting down. Butches evoked the same feelings if I saw them out in public, a terror and a fascination – how did they become like that? What did their lives look like? And, when I allowed myself to think about it, what did they do in bed together? Was sex between two women even possible? This was in the days before iPhones, when the family computer was in the lounge room and Googling 'lesbians' was all too terrifying.

For a long time I mistook my attraction for anxiety. It was easier to fool myself and others into believing I was anxious than to think that my racing heart, sweaty palms and inability to make eye contact with my friend could be attraction. As for those visible butches, their lives seemed so far away from mine, lives I was sure were dominated by being a lesbian *all the time*. Lesbian sexuality defined them. It created a knot in my stomach and a tingling in my pants. At this time I felt my body, my wheelchair, defined me completely, making all other identities impossible, especially sexual identities.

By chance one day I stumbled across something that would change the way I viewed my disability and galvanise me into the fierce, proud disability activist I am today. I was wheeling down the aisle of my small regional library, past the LGBTI books, which were categorised under 'deviance' – I kid you not – and on to the disability section. I picked up a book called *Exploring Disability: A Sociological Introduction*, which explored the disability rights movement and introduced me to the social model of disability. The social model of disability argues that disability is not a personal problem but a social issue of entrenched systematic discrimination and exclusion of people with non-normative bodies and minds. People's attitudes to disability, and the lack of proper access to buildings, transport and housing options are recontextualised by the social model of disability as inherently social issues. Consequently, I would no longer see a flight of stairs and think *I wish I could walk*; I would see them and question why the architect wasn't required to provide access, and what I could do to advocate for change. I also began to feel connected to other people with disabilities to see our shared experiences and not feel so alone. As Liz Crow writes in her article 'Including All of Our Lives':

> For years now this social model of disability has enabled me to confront, survive and even surmount countless situations of exclusion and discrimination ... It has enabled a vision of ourselves free from the constraints of disability oppression and provided a direction for our commitment to social change. It has played a central role in promoting disabled people's individual self-worth, collective identity and political organisation. I don't think it is an exaggeration to say that the social model has saved lives.[1]

With this new political understanding of my body and a hope for a more just world, I began to search out online spaces that were political about disability, such as the BBC's *Ouch* blog. Around this time I also made a friend offline who had a disability, and we would discuss our emerging disability identities and disability pride. This friendship, combined with my online reading and engagement, was critical in enabling me to slowly reframe what it means to have a disability: from an experience of shame and isolation to one of connection and pride.

I gradually learnt how to reconnect with my body, assisted by these politics and a healthy collection of sex toys. Through my reading and discussions, as well as wanking, I taught myself that my body was valuable and desirable. I've had two lovers with disabilities and this has helped change how I see my body. I learnt there was pride to be found in difference. Over time disability would become attractive and desirable in myself and others. I would look at non-normative bodies and find them sexier, more interesting, than those that were 'common' or 'normal'. I began valuing and desiring disabled people, our perspectives and our bodies. I began to call this body home and to do so with pride and passion.

The first time I slept with someone with a body like mine, it was both confronting and profoundly moving. Confronting because I finally saw how my body moved differently during sex, how it reacted to sensation with the whole of its self, how my feelings were entwined with my muscles. *Is that what my body looks like in the throes of orgasm?* I found myself thinking as I watched her. I tried not to cry, not because I was ashamed anymore but because I had never seen it, and because she was so damn beautiful. When you have never seen bodies like yours being sexual, there is power in finally seeing it, and even more power in finding it fucking hot!

I wanted my bedroom to mirror my disability pride and sense of connection to the disability rights movement.

I began to search out images of people with non-normative bodies online, print them out and plaster my walls with them. This would be a place where difference was valued and desired. Among the sexy images lining my wall were some of my idols from the disability rights movement, disability feminists such as Rosemarie Garland-Thomson, Patty Berne, Jenny Morris and Carol Thomas. As they adorned my walls I felt supported and part of the disability rights movement: there was power and pride in a shared experience of non-normativity and the fight for social justice. I was not alone or 'wrong' anymore. I was beautiful in this body, just the way it was.

As I grew to love my body and feel pride in my difference, I was also able to embrace my dormant butch identity and come out. I was still living in a small country town where the local lesbian population consisted of a small group of women who were all interconnected in some fashion, through what is commonly known as the lesbian web. My dabblings in the web caused heartache as I was never cool enough, or maybe I just hadn't had enough sex to be able to have sex without having feelings – plus anyone who comes from a small town will know that it's impossible not to see people out and about with their new love or one-night stand.

I was often excluded from being part of the queer scene because parties were at inaccessible venues, but I was also excluded because of the ideas people held about my disability and my fuckability. One memorable comment that captures this was when a girl I was keen on said, 'You would have been hot if it wasn't for your disability' – as though my disability fundamentally stripped me of desirability. I was, to my knowledge, the only queer woman with a disability in the village, and often people didn't understand my disability or my pride in being different.

Almost four years ago I moved away, to Melbourne – mostly because I needed a change, but in part because I had heard of a queer disability performance troupe called Quippings and I thought, *Those are my people! I want to be where they are!* I was right: they are my people, a small but invaluable group of queer crips who also live the intersections I experience and do so proudly, boldly and unashamedly – and with a bit of flair! I have been performing in and co-producing Quippings for the past two-and-a-half years. We stage shows in and around Melbourne for the Midsumma and Fringe festivals. All our shows deal with themes of disability and sexuality, disability pride and identity. Having a creative means of exploring and expressing my disability and queer identity on stage, in what is often a humorous, sexy and political fashion, has been empowering.

It is still not easy living with multiple marginalities and coming up against ableism and homophobia again and again in their myriad forms. It is a struggle, but these days I am not alone in the struggle: there are others alongside me advocating for change, for our human rights, and calling their bodies home with pride.

As disability and trans activist Eli Clare proclaims on his blog:

I am looking for friends and allies, communities where gawking, gaping, staring finally turns to something else, something true to the bone. Places where strength is softened and tempered, love honed and stretched. Where gender is more than a simple binary. Places where we encourage each other to swish and swagger, limp and roll, and learn the language of pride. Places where our bodies become home.[2]

PEOPLE WHO DELIBERATELY HAD MENSTRUAL SEX WERE MORE OPEN TO OTHER KINDS OF SEX, WERE MORE OFTEN ECSTATIC ABOUT THE RELATIONSHIP THEY WERE IN, AND – HERE'S THE BIG ONE – WERE MORE LIKELY TO FEEL SUCCESSFUL IN COMMUNICATING ABOUT SEX WITH THEIR PARTNERS.

IT GETS MESSY,
AND MAYBE IT SHOULD

ROSANNA BEATRICE

In 2011, academic Dr Breanne Fahs set a group assignment for her undergraduate gender-studies class at Arizona State University: to go out into the world and disrupt it by announcing the presence of periods. While some groups distributed free tampons at a petrol station, or walked Arizona Mall with bloody stains visibly smeared up the crotch of their pants, one collection of students stood on the side of the roads bordering their university campus, and held up signs that read: 'Honk if you love menstrual sex.' Some drivers tooted, others rolled up their windows in avoidance, and a local state representative called the office of the president of the university, demanding to know why students would engage in such sign-bearing obscenity.[1]

Here's what science tells us about the obscenity of periods: there are over 300 different proteins found in menstrual blood that are not found in circulatory human blood. Proteins that, according to research, have the potential to lead wound-healing science, and might reveal a lot about possible cures for endometriosis – a currently unsolvable chronic disease that affects one in ten women in Australia. Analysis of menstrual blood shows that it also contains high levels of a particular stem cell that can morph into other cells – such as nerve cells, which could lead to the development of treatments for stroke and Alzheimer's. All of these 'might's and 'could's exist because the research is still young – there is hope. Menstrual blood is brilliant. Inside the womb it cushions us as we grow into humans who are capable of feeling and contemplating and expressing everything we gorge on as we discover the world. We also know for a tested fact that menstrual blood on a tampon attracts both wild and captive polar bears. Yes, menstruators, that is correct: we can tame the polar bears.[2]

I can't say I learnt about the greatness of periods growing up. Neither did it occur to me, as a teenager, that menstruation and sex could combine – they seemed like oil and water. Which is strange, given all the opportunities I had to learn about menstrual sex. For example, there's that iconic moment in *Fifty Shades of Grey* when Christian Grey pulls a tampon out of Anastasia Steele and has sex with her. Then again, the scene wasn't included in the film because bloody intercourse was too confronting, I guess, for a movie about borderline sexual abuse. But that makes one representation, right?

In hundreds of thousands of hours of porn on the internet, a pornstar is never — not even incidentally — on her, or their, period. This absence is a product of strict laws that prohibit the appearance of blood in porn, to protect industry employees from experiencing bodily harm in their work. I have no place in saying whether these laws are helpful, or only stigmatising, but with the proliferation and popularity of consensual dominance and sadism — from consensually enacted rape fantasies to a more generally accepted slapping, pulling and choking of women in porn — there does seem to be a stark inequality: porn can be consensually violent so long as it's not bloody, but it can't be consensually bloody and violenceless. When I searched for porn with periods in it, the first result was menstrual fetish porn, wherein two women had really slappy sex while litres of fake blood were poured over them on a wet-looking bed, on a set with no other furniture. It was very vampiric and impractical.

Only after specifically searching for simple, softcore, unembellished menstrual porn did I come across one woman who has created an entire website dedicated to representing pleasure on her period. Trixie Fontaine lives and works in Seattle, and for over a decade she uploaded photos, videos and live-streaming content to her period-dedicated website, BloodyTrixie.com. While the site is no longer updated, each remaining show, vlog or photo series involves Trixie, solo, enjoying her period: talking about it frankly and showing viewers her used pads, posing in bloodied underpants, or masturbating. In all her vlogs and videos Trixie seems as much a performer as simply herself: honest, intelligent and sincere.

In an essay published in the journal *Spread* and on her blog, Trixie has discussed the politics and legal limitations forged around sex work that represents both pleasure and menstruation. On the BloodyTrixie homepage, she writes:

> Most porn shows us living our sexual lives as though our periods don't exist, sending the message that bleeding is not natural or sexy. I insist that it's every woman's right to be sexual ... no matter HOW messy her pussy!!! Cyclical bleeding can be beautiful, sensual, freeing, fascinating and fun. I hope you enjoy my red gift to you!

She elaborates on the website:

> Leaving menstruation out of porn and lumping graphic sexual depictions of menstruation together with shit and piss reflect and reinforce a primitive backwater ignorance about women and the human body, reinforcing centuries-old myths, suspicions and fears about blood and the function of women's cycles. This type of ignorance is the TRUE obscenity.

I spoke to Trixie briefly once. She seemed like a lone ranger in her profession, and I was interested to understand who her audience was, what they were seeking out, and to learn whether menstrual sex was only a performance for the internet or something she lived personally. She made it clear to me that most of her cam and phone customers and site members were largely male, sure, but it was her view that they were paying to experience human connection – not just sexual release. She added:

> Periods are a litmus test a lot of times for who I'm having sex with: I don't necessarily want to have bloody sex, but whether or not somebody is comfortable with my period says a lot about them and our compatibility. With my wife, it was awesome because she actually was squeamish about blood, but totally stepped up to the plate to shoot my bloody porn and got used to fucking during that time. Just one of many, many things that made/makes me admire her work ethic, openness, and acceptance. I love to try to gross her out, but she's pretty unflappable.

Up until Trixie, I had never seen or read of a real-life person enjoying their sexuality, or being aroused, on their period: it had seemed like a myth. I had read about non-menstruating people (mainly men) – called Bloodhounds – who were particularly aroused by having sex with menstruating people. Most articles implied, however, that menstruators willingly received sex but didn't actively seek it out. It was the Bloodhounds who took and had the pleasure: the pleasure of the menstruator seemed nearly irrelevant.

But periods aren't just a fetish – they are an unavoidable and biological necessity.

To be honest, I was too old to have *Fifty Shades* as a raunchy seminal text. As a teenager I learnt about periods from tampon ads, which were phenomenally sexy. And I learnt about sex – whether I should do it, how to be sexy, who wanted sex and whether I should want sex – from almost anything that wasn't a tampon ad. When it came time to insert my first tampon, I felt inexplicably dirty – as though I was performing a sexual act, and that sexual act was inherently wrong because sex was wrong and periods were wrong and therefore penetrating myself with a plug of cotton to prevent blood from leaking down my legs was also, by logic, wrong. It's unsurprising that there was an unspoken, almost religious rule between my first boyfriend and me that when I had my period we became as genital-free as dolls. Towards the end of our relationship I lied about having my period to avoid sex a phenomenal number of times. If I'd been Pinocchio, at the point we broke up my nose would have been harvestable to manufacture a shipment of IKEA furniture. I don't even know how my ex-boyfriend felt about my period: that's how little we talked about it.

Nearly ten years later, in 2014, I found myself interviewing sex-education teachers, pre-period teenage soccer stars, the editors of *Dolly* and *Girlfriend* magazines, and my mother for an article about contemporary attitudes towards menstruation. Somewhere in the months of interviews a switch flicked in me and periods became normal: normal-normal, not invisible-normal. I was nonchalant about discussing periods in cafes. I tried five different kinds of reusable menstrual products to see which suited me. Friends of friends found me online and told me their crazy period stories, because they knew I would respond by saying 'How did you feel about that?' or 'Well, someone told me this other period story that confirms how wide-spread your experience is,' or 'You bled on an airplane seat for ten steady hours because you were too mortified to get up? Can I include that in an article?'

The following year, a great crimson wave of period positivity washed across print and online media. People started live-tweeting and Instagramming their periods, others painted with menstrual blood or wrote personal essays, and popular magazines enthusiastically recommended sex for easing menstrual cramps. I was extremely doubtful about the last revelation: based on a prior experience, I thought it seemed ridiculous to suggest that orgasms were a useful healing tool.

Right after high school graduation, my friend Kim had told me she would orgasm to abate headaches. Two days later, as the endless acres of time I had after exams came into view, I inserted a DVD of *Gilmore Girls* into the television and a tendril of ache wormed its way somewhere between my brain and my right eye. I smiled. *A little headache!* I thought to myself as I left the opening credits rolling to the tune of Carole King, and sauntered into my bedroom. *A practice headache.* Perhaps I didn't languish enough – I was too determined to experience the orgasmic outcome, so the whole process of masturbation was as businesslike as a handshake – but as I lay back on a pillow and waited for the rush of brain chemicals to work their easing magic, an ice-burning pain like a length of a rope began to sear its bind around my head.

There is a science to all of this. In 2012 a study by a group of neurological researchers at the University of Münster in Germany found that a portion of migraine and cluster headache patients gained relief from their pain after orgasming – but only a portion. Out of 106 migraine patients who had an orgasm, around sixty saw an improvement in their pain, and around thirty experienced a worsening.[3] Numerous media outlets covered the research findings by proclaiming that the ailed were finally liberated: it seemed sex could absolve headaches. But if you read that sentence again, it *seemed* sex *could* absolve headaches. Based on another study where one in five migraine sufferers said they were 'completely cured' of their pain after having sex, *Cosmopolitan* magazine announced, 'Study Shows That Sex Cures Migraines'. In fact, studies also suggest orgasms can *trigger* headaches – which makes orgasms as pain relief a fun personal game of Russian roulette to very literally try your hand at sometime.

I am yet to find a study conducted to prove that sex effectively relieves menstrual pain. Sure, when you have sex there is an increase in endorphins and corticosteroids in your body, which are key components in experiencing pain relief. Absolutely, if you're having penetrative sex, you can shorten your period. And people of all genders rave about how incomparable menstrual lubrication is – with and without protection. But perhaps the reason why these articles exist isn't just in the name of half-arsed science. Perhaps it's because a lot of readers are like teenage me: we cannot possibly believe that periods and sex can combine in a positive way. These articles offer a reason – a *scientific* reason – for menstruators to allow ourselves to seek out and enjoy period sex.

In 2011 Dr Fahs also conducted a study where she interviewed forty women about how they felt about period sex. Twenty-five participants didn't like the idea and, among complaints about how annoying it was to clean period sex up, one of the reasons that menstruators were deterred from having period sex was dealing with the shame and emotional labour attached to managing their own disgust, and a sexual partner's disgust. But the thirteen women who felt positively about menstrual sex told Dr Fahs that they received physical and emotional pleasure from sex while menstruating, because they didn't give a damn about anti-period attitudes.[4]

This is where things get really interesting: in 2015 the online magazine *Autostraddle* published the results of a survey about menstrual sex that they conducted with over 8,000 members of their readership. You know the clearest thing their feedback revealed? Compared to period-sex rejecters, people who deliberately had menstrual sex were more open to other kinds of sex, were more often ecstatic about the relationship they were in, and – here's the big one – were more likely to feel successful in communicating about sex with their partners. All of this led to a much higher level of satisfaction – sexually and more generally – among those who were in favour of menstrual sex, as opposed to those who were strongly against it.[5] Unsurprisingly, Dr Fahs's research similarly found that women who engaged in menstrual sex also had more partner support than those who avoided menstrual sex.

Meanwhile, at the University of Groningen in the Netherlands, scientists were discovering that sexually aroused women rated activities deemed 'icky' – like drinking water with a bug in it, or wiping hands on a used tissue – as much less gross compared to women who were not aroused.[6] Perhaps the real mess of menstrual sex, then, is that to have it, or to think about it, or to talk about it, we have to confront ourselves. Instead of simply being awkward or disgusted – which are such normalised and easy reactions to have towards the idea of period sex – we have to sit with our embarrassment or our deepest objections, and think them through. We each have the opportunity to listen to the conservative local state representative in our head, protesting that menstrual sex is an obscenity. We also have the opportunity to confront whatever fears we have about period sex in our own time, and come to a thoughtful conclusion about it.

When I read all of these studies, my first reaction wasn't relief or celebration. I was daunted – my girlfriend and I didn't have a lot of menstrual sex. In a pie chart, or an academic study, would we be part of the doomed percentage? Was I supposed to seek pleasure and feel liberated while I bled, like Trixie Fontaine? In a way, I wanted to be able to. I like the idea of being irreverent towards social expectations surrounding menstruation; however, like everyone, personal experiences all through my life have conditioned my relationships to both sex and periods. I like the idea of simply shrugging off the weight of all that weirdness and having really noisy, sanguine orgasms. I want to prove the Dutch science right and kick over any private grossness I feel towards my period because I am too turned on to care about whether or not I am bleeding while I have sex.

When my girlfriend and I do have red sex, it is usually an accident: we might discover one of us has our period in the middle of intercourse, or at the end. If one of us discovers our period just as we begin to have sex, we usually make an assessment. 'Are you going to be okay?' the non-menstruating girlfriend asks the menstruating girlfriend. The other might respond with, 'Quick! Quick! Just get a towel! Before it starts properly!' I admit we have been vaguely concerned about stains: it *does* gets messy. Maybe it should. But sometimes after sex we want to snuggle and nap instead of re-making a bed and putting uterine lining in the washing hamper.

It's not that simple, though. We're not afraid of periods – when one of us asks the other 'Are you going to be okay?' it's because we're afraid of pain. Our concern is always rooted in a fear of how unbearably achy our periods might become, and whether that ache might be worsened by sex. My girlfriend has dysmenorrhoea, or painful periods. I have endometriosis – a chronic disease of the uterus and abdominal area – that is most excruciating during menstruation. The last thing either of us wants to feel during the deep end of our heaviest days is sexual. Nothing pleases my girlfriend more than feeling sorry for herself and having someone massage her back. I only wish to lie as still as possible and experience facial tingling from high-strength painkillers.

Still, I worried we didn't fit into the statistically successful portion of period-radical sex-positive relationships that recent research had proven existed. Was our pain a farce? Were we actually conservative and judgemental about menstrual sex? I stopped writing this essay, burst into our sitting room and sat beside my girlfriend to debrief. Here's how the conversation went:

Me: Would you like to have sex tonight?
Girlfriend: Oh – I have my period, babe. Day two. I really don't feel like it.
Me: I know. But do you want to have more period sex?
Girlfriend: I mean, we do have period sex sometimes. At the beginning, or the end of our cycles. Is this because

of the piece you're writing at the moment?

Me: Yes.

Girlfriend: Do you want to have sex tonight?

Me: Well, all this research says that perhaps we should be having more period sex.

Girlfriend: Yes, but do you *want* to?

Me: I don't really feel like it. Generally. I have heaps to do tonight.

Girlfriend: Do you want us to have sex more on *your* period?

Me: It just gets so painful. I feel like *The Exorcist* is actually an account of my uterus shedding its lining.

Girlfriend: Okay, but you know you could always come to me. If you wanted to taste my menstrual blood, we could talk about that.

Me: Well, you know there's a new study that says you're less disgusted by things when you're aroused.

Afterwards, I wondered what would have happened if I'd spoken about period sex with my first boyfriend – my Pinocchio boyfriend. Perhaps, recognising I wasn't attracted to him anymore, I would have ended our relationship sooner. Maybe we would have talked about my menstrual pain and, agreeing it was uncharacteristically terrible, gone to the doctor, where I would have been diagnosed with endometriosis seven years earlier than I was.

What I know with certainty is that, compared to my Pinocchio relationship, I am now someone who is unafraid to talk to others, and to advocate for myself and what I believe is normal. I'm in a relationship with a partner who understands the importance of communicating about sex and desire, about plans to live overseas, and about whose responsibility the laundry hamper is. Like the *Autostraddle* survey suggested, satisfaction comes from communication. We don't need to be *having* menstrual sex, but we do need to be in relationships – with ourselves and with others – where we can think and talk about it. Because the only thing that should sit in the way of me having menstrual sex is me.

I WILL COME WITH HER NAME
CAUGHT IN THE BACK OF MY THROAT,
AND FEEL IT RUN THROUGHOUT MY
LIMBS, MY BLOOD QUICKENING WITH
EACH SYLLABLE PULSE.

GASP uNDER GASP, SIGH BEHIND SIGH

TILLY LAWLESS

'For you alone I reserve that Gasp under Gasp, that Sigh behind Sigh, that Attention back of feigned' – Djuna Barnes

There's nothing like waking up and sculling a litre of pineapple juice before breakfast to be ready to pee on a man's face. Morning sex has never been my thing but here I am, fucking on an empty stomach.

People sometimes ask if it becomes hard to differentiate sex in my private life from sex at work. There is nothing like sex with someone you love, and no amount of orgasming with a client ever makes them feel less like a client, or lessens the orgasms with my girlfriend. Sex with Dani is never a chore, never at a pre-determined time, never when I don't feel like it – three defining aspects of work. It's not like the genuineness and love of my private life are somehow pared away with each work exchange; if anything the chasm between sex for love and sex for work is made even more glaring, and makes me appreciate what I have all the more.

I have been drawn out of her bed by the allure and promise of green, the ka-ching of cash louder than the clack of my stilettos on wood as I pace away the remaining minutes to his arrival. I leave her bed so as to pay for the downtime to stay in her bed, sleep-tousled and wet-thighed, for days upon days. Watch movies and smoke weed and make her come till the room is musty with sex and there is a thin layer of white on the sheets that I can scritch off with a thumbnail when it dries. It's 8.45 am and usually I would only be pressing my arse against her in a desperate sleepy need to feel her hands upon my waist, but now I am readying myself to sit on a stranger's cock and hoping my bloated bladder does not burst too soon.

It was easier to work when I was single. No other bed called me besides the brothel bed. Now I cancel and complain and peel off notes reluctantly, showing none of the eager abandon with which I strip for her. Clothes can be simply – and hopefully never – put back on. That $100 has to be re-earned. Is $500 really worth leaving the heavy-aired, tucked-beneath-your-armpit space that I so love to nestle in? I know I've seen *Bridget Jones's Diary* five times already but I am loath to leave it now. When you love someone the most mundane task can seem special – you can share a cigarette or a meal that is more intimate than anything else. So to leave that hazy place of muffled sounds, those 'mmmms' and 'mmmmyeahs' that crinkle the corners of my eyes and leave my heart pressed up against my ribcage, is hard. I drag my feet and wish my hair would drag too, grow and twist till it caught on her bedstead and trapped me there beyond my control. Why can't I stay?

I am leaving so as to come back, I tell myself.

It is a harsh capitalist truth that we must pay even for our free time, and so now I go to fund our sloth.

The client is here. He is a nice man with an even nicer dick, and I orgasm happily. Among all the men who shipwreck themselves on the rocks of my anatomy, I occasionally meet one that I readily come with. What at first confused me I now simply see as a bonus, and as the lube runs down my legs I am satisfied. We move to the shower, where I lower my pussy over his mouth and he sucks up my pee straight from the source, his pursed lips reminiscent of a teenage me sculling goon, or the oddly intimate movement of a friend drinking the nectar from a honeysuckle. I feel ever giving and wish I had more of the sweetened urine to give, endless amounts to splash over his open-mouthed, curved-eyed bliss.

'So do you have a boyfriend?' he asks, in the contented aftermath of sex. When time is still left in the booking and we lie on the bed together, relishing the peace of the allocated time before we have to rush back into the day.

'No, I have a girlfriend.' And I think of her, winking at me as she fakes orgasm over the mouth of another man, holding in her laugh as I turn a yawn into a moan at 2.00 am, pulling me in to breathe 'I love you' against my lips while the client furiously masturbates, oblivious. Who can ever plumb those depths; who can understand that which fits no mould except that of our own creating?

As he leaves, Dani calls me. 'He had a really nice dick and I orgasmed,' I say in the same tone I would say 'he was super chill'. It is a non-event, this orgasm. Later today she will plaster my sweating mess of a body against the bedsheets as she grinds a strap-on into the very epicentre of me, and it will not be those quakes that obliterate any other orgasm from my mind but the things that lead up to them throughout the day. The tenderness and respect and divulging of truths. I will come with her name caught in the back of my throat, and feel it run throughout my limbs, my blood quickening with each syllable pulse.

What is a sexual interaction compared with the reality we live together every day? She sees me cry and laugh and fume, she sees me flounce off in irritation, she sees me impassioned and moody. I have opened my legs to clients but there is no real knowing there. No background to the snapshot they have of me, almost a disembodied person in an out-of-context frame. A soulless work apartment, empty except for fucking. They have not packed me a cone when I can't sleep, nor pulled me to when scared and lonely.

I watch her roll the condom on now, harness tight upon her haunches, and she grins at me. We both know. There is not even the thought of another to slip between us and harden a nipple with ghostly cold. 'Mmmmm,' I encourage, as she bends down.

I EXIST AND FEEL DESIRE.
THESE ARE UNIVERSAL STATEMENTS
THAT CAN BE APPLIED TO EVERYONE
AND SOMETIMES THERE'S PHOTOGRAPHIC
EVIDENCE OF BOTH.

SEXT AND STIMULATION

AMY GRAY

It's roughly seven seconds between messages. We start small – asking about each other's lives, his record or his tour, my book or my article. In between messages, I scour my bedroom; there's life to hide.

You can do your eyeliner in seven seconds.

You can do your mascara in the next seven.

By the time you've shared five minutes of pleasantries, you're on the bed in rehearsed lingerie with an 'I lounge around like this all the time' look that's ready for action – for sharing photos.

The thought crosses my mind that it's one-sided. Women often bear the expectation of holding the male gaze aloft – of beds with no laundry on them, eyes dewy with the still-dissipating fumes of makeup. Even when you're not at home, you're maintaining that gaze with artful composure, hiding the suitcase in your hotel room.

Meanwhile, he's taking photos in public toilets and dressing rooms.

He was a chance encounter, fifty metres from my door and on tour with his band. He was brutish and halting, with scraggly long hair and beard – a wolf out of place. 'Women are afraid of me because I look like a Viking,' he told me. With his long hulking frame, he stooped himself – 'I'm shy.'

He really wasn't, though.

By the time he flew back home to Paris, I had accompanied him through the hills of Italy, shitty bars in Berlin and the wilds of Russia. All through our phones, a secret in our back pockets. We spun elaborate stories for each other: scenarios in airport cupboards, rotten New York alleys and flaking apartments in Paris.

In a shared story, anything is possible – he can twist your bound, hanging body from a hook, you can suddenly deepthroat with ease, he can fuck for hours at a time, and you don't need to train your arse for anal.

After our stories, we would spin together softer tales – of lying in bed, drinking coffee and smoking. Or lazily squabbling over monster movies as though we had collapsed naked onto one another on the couch, waiting for pizza to arrive. We would trash-talk about whose cat was prettier. Thousands of miles apart, and I could smell the beer on his breath and feel his beard tickling my neck.

Endorphins can be tricked. On the days my inbox filled with a hundred emails containing stories and photos, my body unfurled into the deepest bliss. I knew his skin on a cellular level despite not being able to touch him.

We had committed our ephemeral bodies to memory so comprehensively that they felt closer than they were. Our carefully shot photos in the beginning, that slow unveiling of our curves and angles, always hid our faces, but I knew his chest – every strand of its hair and the way his pecs would shape. I knew his cock intimately – every ripple when soft, every vein when hard.

When the body can be fooled, so can the heart if it hears the same script often enough. He lied and said he missed me, I lied and said I would visit. We weren't in a relationship, but there was a bond, a shared delusion as we played our roles.

In kink, roles are contained and exhaustively negotiated. In relationships, there is hopefully enough talking to find your own, slipping into your part as you wake. But when the person you desire is thousands of miles from you, out of step in different times and zones, those roles are more quietly guided from the stories you share and the emails you ignore. Basic programming to show you what will get a response and what won't.

Play your role often enough, watching keenly for feedback, and you become an adept actor, taking notes from your performance to find meaning and direction to the point you forget you're even on a stage – an artificial set cobbled together from boredom, loneliness and need.

'What are you doing right now?': *I'm bored.* 'I miss you': *I'm lonely.* 'You mean so much to me': *It's easier talking to a screen than a real person.* Together we became props to each other's performances – performed on separate stages, to separate scripts to an audience of none.

Yet reality intruded, the bright lights clunked on during an intermission between acts, ushers guiding us back to reality. Perhaps we needed details to explain the reasons the other would disappear, or that desire to see their whole selves rather than disconnected parts in all those secret photos. That need to see the breasts that swelled and the pleading eyes that followed the tug of a cock. An expanded intimacy to amplify the performance. It required trust and we still hadn't even agreed to share our surnames with each other.

We agreed that we would share two details about ourselves, and let the other find us. I had found him weeks before, but kept quiet about that fact. He had a blue tick on Twitter and a Wikipedia entry. Hundreds and thousands of fans would hit 'like' on his public photos. We both had wide trails for the other to find.

Despite our words of communion and rituals of confirmation, we never acknowledged each other publicly. There were no friend requests, no online validation. Instead, he would occasionally post photos of himself in Australia, wishing he was back here, and I started tweeting about French politics.

We existed as a continually orbiting but distant connection – together in private, apart in public and in actuality.

In real time, itself a nod to our transience, I sat through the terrorist attacks and recording-label fights with him; he sat through my hospital appointments, muggings, and the deaths of friends. Invisibly present, never claiming this as a relationship, and never fully existing or trusting.

But the choice to share our real identities made us trust each other more. We switched from a messaging app to email, our actual private email addresses. The conversations stayed the same but the photos we shared became more intense. Not from how we positioned ourselves, but because we included our faces, presenting our whole selves. Eyes betray an intimacy more than anything else can, from wide-eyed bafflement to fire to something that skimmed close to affection.

It was never discussed – those words were reserved for the stories we would share with each other – but we had moved on to a new intimacy. Not one where you curl into another at 3.00 am and confess your fragilities, hoping for acceptance; but one where you willingly display your desire, trusting it will never be thrown out to the world.

Trust, however, is a tension that hit us with surprising equality. When a man's naked photos are publicly released, there is very rarely a ripple. His pursuit of desire is judged as natural, an act accepted with affection and humour – those boys being boys. He knew, though, that his photos would be judged the same as a woman's.

When a woman's naked photos are publicly released, her desire is seen as an indictment, a crime to have shown her needs in a society expecting her to fulfil everyone's but her own. Men can show desire – society caters to their needs as natural events – but a woman can only show herself responding to male desire, her desires pointedly ignored. We want women to be sexually pleasing, not sexual – to admit sexuality is to admit an independent hunger, a profound want. Such an admission renders us whole, complex figures – more than slabs of flesh available for male moulding and profit.

His celebrity, however, brought him down from the normal male invulnerability and closer to my status as woman: a two-dimensional image, constructed with no meaning or motivation other than to please the viewer. Perhaps his relative fame promised mutually assured destruction, a bomb neither of us wanted to detonate. Even so, society will accept his body in all it does, more than it ever will mine; though a man can bare his cock out in public and have a cheeky slash without censure, a woman can barely expose a breast to feed that same man's child. Man is allowed function, while woman is reduced to form.

If our photos ever leaked, people would call it 'revenge porn'. While others decry the term as a euphemism that hides the often gendered crime, it feels like the perfect descriptor to me, because it shows how we cast women as objects for male pleasure and penalty. Having sexted for a decade, I insist on men sexting back photos of themselves – it is as much insurance as it is insistence they conform to my gaze as well. Let them run to the mirror to check their face, to their bedroom to hide their mess; let them reduce themselves to trusting body parts that are seeking approval for my desire and acceptance.

I am not some mute meal for noiseless consumption. I am not a compliant program seeking to run through all variables until it reaches its successful conclusion of a man's fingers glistening with his come. I may live in a world that demands I protect men's secrets while presenting my own as objects for sale or trade, but that doesn't mean I'm above upending a few tables to interrupt the market.

As the years (and men) have rolled on, I have lost the fear of someone releasing naked photos of me. Perhaps he could share the photos and stories that lie sleeping in his inbox, those dormant, forgotten pleasures, if he ever feels the need for 'revenge'. But how could someone claim vengeance on me by releasing my photos?

I exist and feel desire. These are universal statements that can be applied to everyone and sometimes there's photographic evidence of both.

So why would I feel ashamed to have my desire outed? The presumption of shame would suggest I hold my desire as less natural than a man's, that my desired body should be hidden from view unless a man can work out how to make a buck from it. Shame would blindfold me from the most exquisite irony afflicting all sexting shamers and revenge-porn cockroaches: they continually search for photos of naked women to excite themselves, only to call women ugly.

Nothing about this is new. There is no shock in displaying what the world says I must deny and yet secretly hopes will be stolen from me. When women are on a public platform, the unspoken negotiation is they must silence their voice and present their bodies for inspection.

There are intersections within this – women are examined based on their race, size and ability – but the net result is that we're inspected and judged as two-dimensional; not afforded the same share of acceptance given to men, but expected to carry all of the penalty for their power and desire. When our proudly vulnerable photos of our naked bodies are seen, it's demanded we shrink from that platform rather than what we should do: double down and demand the world accept that we are as complex and forgivable as men.

So here I am. It's not the first topless photo you've seen; it won't be the last. Others will be equally assured, legs firming against any shove off the platform. We construct society and desire – the only thing that is real is my refusal.

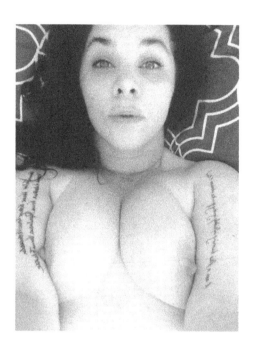

POP MUSIC TEACHES YOU WHAT
LUST IS MEANT TO FEEL LIKE,
LONG BEFORE YOU ACTUALLY FEEL IT.

WILDEST DREAMS: POP-MUSIC CRUSHES AND PRE-TEEN SEX POSITIVITY

SINEAD STUBBINS

From the time that young women are old enough to engage with pop culture (in the womb? slipping out of the birth canal?) the idea that you are required to have a celebrity crush is paramount to your pop-culture literacy. Sometimes this social requirement arrives before you're ready – I recall inspecting the video for Sixpence None the Richer's 'Kiss Me' and following the lyrics (provided by *TV Hits*, my god what a resource) with all the intensity of an archaeologist studying an ancient relic for clues to understanding a far-off existence. Why was this girl so obsessed with the clothes she would be wearing and the place she would be standing when she was kissed? Why was Freddie Prinze Jr there?

But later on, you get it. You *get* it. You are just another in a long line of women throughout history who have worshipped a pop star, who have experienced crying, aching adoration and projected giant pink neon hearts of energy into the atmosphere. You are the reincarnation of girls in 1957 screaming louder than Elvis can sing, while scandalised men in hats frown and secretly fear that they've lost control of this realm. You are the shivering girl waiting at the airport in 1964, praying to get a glimpse of John, Paul, George and Ringo because they understood you and wanted to talk to you and thought you were worthy of their songs. You're the young women who jumped up from their seats in shock in 1983, when Michael Jackson began gliding across the stage in his first moonwalk. And when you die, there will still be young women gathered in stadiums (in space?) shouting praise at men who know the secret codes to opening their hearts.

This has always been a space where you don't have to worry that it's not 'proper' to be a screaming, craving sexual being. Beautiful boys with real nice hair encourage girls to look at and project fantasies on them, creating art that makes the girl's needs paramount (albeit art that makes heterosexual needs paramount). Pop-music crushes can set the tone for how you see yourself and your sexuality, a kind of test run where there's no pressure to be or act a certain way. Pop-music moments become the markers for how you measure time.

(1997: Hanson release 'MMMBop' and even heterosexual men fall in love with a teenage boy so beautiful that he looks like an angel from a Renaissance painting.)

As it's a thing that young women like, however, pop music is often trivialised as not being a legitimate artform – because teenage girls couldn't possibly be legitimate tastemakers. Thankfully the democratisation of the internet means that the old caste of pop-hating, crusty male music critics is being drowned out by other voices who mock this traditional pop-hate as clichéd. The cynical view that pop is manufactured to trigger feelings of love in young women – so that they will dutifully buy albums and merchandise – suggests that girls have no agency in the matter, when it's the girls who make these musicians stars. Sometimes it's because the music is incredible, sometimes it's because the musician is incredible, and sometimes it's both. Maybe you only listen to 5 Seconds of Summer because they've got a cute social media presence, or maybe your love of One Direction started when you saw how funny they are in interviews. Who cares?

(2015: Harry Styles grabs Niall Horan's crotch after winning Best Duo/Group at the Billboard Music Awards; millions of teenagers spontaneously black out.)

Here, Laura Mulvey's 'male gaze' is suddenly inverted: women are told that we are the ones who must watch, and these male pop idols, who dance, wink and smile at us, are the ones to be watched. The pop star looks at us looking at them, and is comfortable with the imbalance of power (the true difference between pop stars and rock bands with legions of female fans: the pop stars don't think it's a bad thing that their demographic is mostly female). This is a realm where all notions of gendered respectability evaporate. Expressing a howling (emotional/sexual) longing is not only appropriate, it's encouraged. Even as a seven-year-old watching the video for George Michael's 'Fastlove' I concluded: *oh, this must be what sexiness is.* Pop music teaches you what lust is meant to feel like, long before you actually feel it. Years before, poor George Michael had to repeatedly justify naming a song 'I Want Your Sex', assuring scandalised American VJs that it was just about monogamous love and wasn't too racy for his young listeners, *really.* The fact that One Direction's Harry Styles now has a 'Careless Whisper' tattoo on his person is almost too perfect, a meta-pop reference that echoes teen thirst throughout the ages.

(1986: Wham! play their final concert at Wembley Stadium in London and 72,000 people attend, marking the most earnest event in Britain's history.)

The 1990s was the epoch of the boyband wave and the last decade in which five dudes wearing matching outfits while performing matching dances was considered attractive. We had British and Irish boys – like Take That, East 17, Boyzone, 5ive and Westlife – along with their slicker, more successful American counterparts Boyz II Men,

98 Degrees, the Backstreet Boys and NSYNC. By the end of the '90s, NSYNC were the biggest boyband in the world; they seemed younger than the Backstreet Boys and more willing to engage with futuristic EDM (electronic dance music), which dominated the Y2K zeitgeist, while also being edgy enough to have Nelly rap an interlude on their 2002 hit 'Girlfriend'. And, of course, from NSYNC was born Justin Timberlake.

(2003: Justin Timberlake releases the video for his single 'Cry Me a River', which is allegedly about Britney Spears cheating on him. The video involves him breaking into her house, and watching her shower. She is still miraculously the bad guy.)

Justin Timberlake's career has been built on telling girls that they deserve better. His persistent image of the fantasy boyfriend embodies the fantasy of basic respect. Since joining NSYNC at fifteen, Timberlake has presented as the good boy with bad ideas. His first *Rolling Stone* cover story included him repeatedly saying how much he loved his mother, how all of his girlfriends had cheated on him and how he was still in love with Britney (their relationship had coincided with her strict and unfortunate 'I'm still a virgin' marketing campaign, which earned him extra points for being 'respectful' – even when he very publicly put her on blast in a music video for cheating on him). His vulnerability and openness about his heartbreak was his superpower, crafting an image where young girls thought of him as a safe option, albeit one who would show them a real nice time.

When Justin Timberlake went solo with 2002's *Justified*, his Timbaland- and Neptunes-produced tracks may have sounded more sophisticated, but his musical sentiment was the same: he still wanted to save the hot girl from the bad relationship. He may have shaved off his baby curls and bought a hoodie (the suits would come later) but he was still the same Justin. His music progressed from wanting to fulfil women's emotional needs to also wanting to fulfil their sexual needs. In 'Senorita' he wants to know why a beautiful girl is crying, admonishing the man she's with for not giving her the crown she deserves. In 'Sexyback' he swivels between flexing and saying that he knows how to treat a girl nice (the other boys don't, you see), and being completely subservient and offering himself up to be whipped. Justin Timberlake wants to listen to you talk about your feelings, and he doesn't mind if you want him to wear handcuffs *while* he's listening.

Justin Timberlake isn't in the teen-idol zeitgeist anymore, but the fans who have grown up with him still carry the same projections from their teens. At his 2013 MTV Video Music Awards Vanguard performance, which comprised a fifteen-minute medley of his greatest hits, he invited NSYNC on stage to rapturous applause. Timberlake knows that his roots lie in stadiums of howling teenagers, and he's not ashamed of it. In the audience, Taylor Swift and Selena Gomez screamed. One Direction clapped politely.

If Justin Timberlake shows how the 'old school' pop idol can evolve with his fans, then it took another singing and dancing Justin to prove that young girls can make and preserve a career. Justin Bieber, YouTube prodigy, already had an existing fan base of Beliebers (who initially drew comparisons to Beatlemania but were soon overshadowed by the Directioners' obsession with those British ragamuffins) before he signed a record deal in 2008. His early songs were full of vague longing, a fifteen-year-old singing to thirteen-year-olds about undying love that they hadn't felt yet. It was no secret who he was making music for; every song was for his 'Favourite Girl' or the 'One Less Lonely Girl' he'd pull out of the audience, or the 'Baby' that had broken his heart. The most popular boy in school was sensitive, and he noticed you in the corner.

(2010: Justin Bieber accounts for 3 per cent of all traffic on Twitter. Sadly, it is also the year that Lady Gaga wears her meat dress.)

The Beliebers started to get older and suddenly being someone's 'Favourite Girl' wasn't enough. Music critics began saying that Bieber was pulling a Timberlake by choosing more sophisticated R&B hooks and dirty dancing with Nicki Minaj in videos. In 2012 he sang at the Victoria's Secret Fashion Show and the reaction from the models made it clear: Justin was growing up. Of course, like many pop stars who are thrust into stardom before puberty, Justin Bieber's world started to cave in on him. He made bad choices, was arrested a few times, and was booed at the 2013 Billboard Awards while winning their Milestone gong at nineteen. He became a joke. The Beliebers waited.

Then, in 2015, their prayers were answered. A new Justin Bieber emerged, a little more guarded, more wary about the public's perception of him, and – as it turned out – a lot more ripped. Bieber became your on-again-off-again boyfriend with whom you have a torrid *Notebook*-style relationship but who you just can't shake – hell, even Selena Gomez broke up and reunited with him several times, releasing a song called 'The Heart Wants What It Wants' about his relentless hold on her.

He attracted critical success, but young girls don't need their tastes legitimised by old white men who write album reviews offline – Bieber was speaking to *them*. 'What Do You Mean' is a song about dramatic relationships, but could be interpreted as a song about consent. 'Love Yourself' is about being led astray by the wrong person. 'Sorry' reads as an apology to every girl he has ever let down, a song so filled with remorse that he didn't even allow himself to be in the video, instead employing an all-female dance troupe to interpret his words. Between Calvin Klein underwear ads and forced contrition on every talk show in existence, Bieber was making amends. Just like his fans, he's still trying to figure out what his boundaries are.

Let's pause for a second. Let's think about how often young women are actually told that what they feel matters. That what they *want* matters. Of course Justin

Timberlake and Justin Bieber are successful because they make catchy music, but you can't disregard how rare it is for girls to feel as seen and heard as they do in the two Justins' music. How often do they get that promise of unconditional love and respect? This is far removed from the indie-rock music I listened to growing up, which was mostly young men singing about beautiful women they'd never get, in songs they hoped other young men would listen to. I knew I should be a 'Taper Jean Girl', or the one who Alex Turner thought looked good on the dance-floor, or the goddess who repeatedly broke Death Cab for Cutie's collective hearts. I wonder how I would have felt if I'd listened to music that told me that I didn't know I was beautiful and, you know, that's kind of what made me beautiful.

(2003: Death Cab for Cutie appear on the Music from the O.C. *soundtrack, attracting a legion of teen girl fans. Indie boys crumble into dust.)*

Of course, it isn't just male musicians who affect their listeners' attitudes towards sex. The big pop wave of the 1990s was dominated by artists like Britney Spears and Christina Aguilera; their sexuality, however, was wielded like something to be flaunted but never enjoyed. Britney Spears was presented as a girl in a woman's body, who was clueless to her own Lolita image. Britney told girls that to act on their impulses was forbidden, literally draping a snake around her neck during a 2001 performance of 'I'm a Slave 4 U', making her temptation seem almost biblical. Christina too was hypersexual, but she never seemed to enjoy it; she was always writhing in cages or boxing rings as if her sexuality was something unruly that needed to be contained. These pop stars were meant to be the logical progression from Madonna, who, despite using her sexuality to shock people, at least advocated that, yes, young women want to have sex just as much as men do. It seems stupid to say this, but this sentiment still isn't always reflected in pop culture. I remember listening to Gwen Stefani's 2004 single 'Bubble Pop Electric' – a song that was genuinely inspired by '80s Madonna – and being shocked to hear her roleplay a scenario where a teen girl calls up her boyfriend (played by André 3000) to suggest that she wants to lose her virginity in the backseat of his car that night. She wasn't even worried about it! She was *asking* him for sex!

Male pop stars can encourage sexual fantasies and imagined emotional relationships that fill your head with fuzz, but it's female pop stars who tell young women: 'what you feel and what you want is *normal*'. Your crushes don't have to be a dark secret. If Madonna used her sexual appetite as rebellion, then the pop stars who normalised an active and aggressive female libido have to be the Spice Girls.

(1997: At the premiere of Spice World: The Movie, *Mel B kisses Prince Charles on the cheek and Geri pinches his butt; the class system in Britain collapses.)*

The Spice Girls aren't remembered for making the 'right' kind of pop. They are criticised for being a silly, hollow marketing construction – something for which female artists are always judged more harshly than male ones. In retrospect, the Spice Girls were revolutionary. They were a breath of fresh air in a stagnant, smoke-filled, lager-drinking Britpop scene where girls were rarely allowed, and they were the biggest pop band of the mid-'90s when boybands were popping up like weeds. When *Top of the Pops* tried to mock them by giving them reductive nick-names – Ginger, Scary, Baby, Posh and Sporty – the girls embraced and reclaimed them.

The Spice Girls were just normal girls. Their first single in 1997, 'Wannabe', was an earworm about the importance of female friendship over men, but the video invoked a kind of class war. The girls crash a party in a fancy hotel, harassing rich people and literally saying 'cor!' and then ending the video by hopping on a double-decker bus. Their songs told girls that they could do anything, not limited to but including demanding that boys step up their game and telling them exactly what they wanted – 'Last Time Lover' is basically an instructional manual for female pleasure. Their songs swung wildly between fury at the ineptitude of boys and breathlessly inviting the real men to come over. The Spice Girls always seemed like they were in control.

In Kathy Acker's infamous 1997 profile on the girls for American *Vogue*, in which she seems totally overwhelmed by their Englishness, the Spice Girls explain that they can relate to their fans because they're underdogs too. They know what it's like to deal with rubbish men. Geri even says that she loves it when fans come up to her saying that the Spice Girls inspired them to break up with their boyfriends. Boys were disposable, but friendship was forever. Even though the Spice Girls and their 'girl power' mantra were mocked for being inauthentic, to young women – the people they were directly speaking to – it was sexual and emotional autonomy handed over in a sequined Union Jack mini-dress.

Girls telling girls that wanting love and sex is okay – that's something powerful. Taylor Swift, in particular, has made a career of telling stories about fairytale romance that allow girls to daydream of finding that kind of love, counterbalanced with tales of disillusionment that remind girls that they are not alone. Famously, Taylor writes about her actual boyfriends and leaves clues in the liner notes about who some songs are about; she is complicit in sparking her fans' imagination. Anecdotal songwriting is praised in men as being authentic and raw; in women it's seen as tacky and exploitative. But Taylor Swift fans know that she's sharing her real stories of heartbreak, longing and redemption, because they have the same stories – but, you know, usually not involving Harry Styles. She articulates the humiliation and rejection that other musicians aren't honest enough to express.

(2014: Taylor Swift releases the satirical video for 'Blank Space', in which she plays a crazed ex-girlfriend and makes it corny for anyone to make jokes about her having a lot of boyfriends ever again.)

The best thing about Taylor's 2014 album *1989* is that she finally seems unafraid to explicitly discuss sexual longing. Songs like 'Wildest Dreams' – which depicts a secret and torrid fling, days of clothes strewn on floors, and all-night, um, tangles – normalise her fans' desires. (Meanwhile, Taylor's best friend Selena Gomez released a song this year called 'Hands to Myself', about masturbation. Their catch-up dinner conversations must be amazing these days.) Through engaging with fans on social media, Taylor reminds you that she's your friend, someone who is just like you. Her storytelling reassures girls, even those who aren't ready to act on their emotional or physical impulses yet, that everything is going to be alright when they do. Like Taylor, they deserve love and respect, and shouldn't be afraid of advocating for themselves.

In 2004 a study in the journal *Personality and Individual Differences* found that, developmentally, avid fandom and obsession with pop idols is very good for pre-teens, encouraging emotional autonomy and providing a safe avenue to explore romantic feelings.[1] By projecting desire onto pop stars, fans can better understand what their desires actually are. The stickers from *TV Hits* may have been replaced by dedicated Tumblrs, but the sentiment is still the same: here is a world that is just for you, where you don't need to feel ashamed for feeling a certain way.

From the first moment a teenage girl screamed at Elvis gyrating on her television set, the cosmos was changed. This is the space where she sheds the too-tight skin of feminine passivity, and can instead express a bold hunger and be pushy, demanding and far too loud. Everything about this experience – the pop star, the music, the thousands of other fans standing beside her – tells her that this is natural. Later on, the object of your affection might not have a perfect fringe or sequined leotard, but your love will be just as pure. Pop stars provide practice love and lust that gets you ready for the real thing. Maybe the foundation for great sex is actually no sex at all.

I AM NOT STILL HAVING SEX WITH THE SAME PERSON. WE'VE BOTH CHANGED SO MANY TIMES. SO MANY.

WHY IT NEVER GETS OLD

JENNA PRICE

I always knew I would enjoy sex.

This was the enduring gift from my hilarious parents, who loved their lives and their children, and passed that on, in just twenty-six years.

I always knew I would enjoy sex just as I always knew I would enjoy food, because this was what happened in my family. In the same way that parents build their kids' ideas around reading or around exercise, they also build their kids' ideas around bodies, around self-esteem – and around pleasure. (This turned out to be much harder when I had to do it myself, but that's another story.)

Our parents always reminded us that sex was fun. There was an explicit comparison between sex and eating; if you were hungry, you should eat! These reminders came often, and even more so as puberty loomed.

We were lucky. My older sister, my younger brother

and I were brought up in a household where sex was okay. Better than okay. It was normal. It was clearly neither painful nor embarrassing to my parents and was occasionally a topic of conversation at the dinner table.

Not icky. Not adultifying. No creepy grown-up was trying to get us to do these things early. Sex was just a regular, enjoyable part of adult life. Something we could look forward to when we were ready.

So this is my story of how I started to have sex, and why and how I enjoyed it from the very beginning to now, nearly fifty years on. It's also a brief rationale of why I try to be an advocate for open discussions of the actual act of sex. And, like sex itself, there will be a bit of a reveal when you get to the end. My own enjoyment of sex meant that I eventually did something that women who are happy with their bodies are never meant to do. Especially not feminists. No. No. No.

There is an extraordinary resistance to discussing sex, unless it's with your doctor. Yes, women are monitored and surveilled when it comes to how they talk about sex, but I don't think men have an easier time. We are all supposed to don our stereotypes when we reveal our intimacies: women, timid and fearful; men, frankly swinging their dicks. We are soft; they are hard.

But I can talk about sex all day long and I blame that on my parents. Not that I knew the details, mind you. I couldn't tell you now if my parents had orgasms when they had sex but, theoretically, they did. And I knew I would, eventually.

Mum and Dad were embarrassingly clear about their enjoyment of each other's bodies and there was always a fair bit of public smooching. There was also the odd bottom pinch, both by Dad of Mum's very capacious bum and by Mum of Dad's rear, which was somewhat less capacious but still obviously a bottom. And there were muscular hugs in the kitchen, in front of the hot stove: hopeless from an occupational health and safety perspective but utterly compelling as role models for young teenagers.

They were, looking back, ostentatiously affectionate.

No, not ostentatious; that's not quite the right word. They were not trying to flaunt their affection; they were merely expressing what they felt, and were uninhibited in the presence of their children. They were not just telling us that they loved each other. They showed us.

Love of course meant more than touching – but the touching made love concrete, made love visible. Patting, pinching, stroking, hugging, squeezing, holding hands. Even in their mid-fifties. All of this was cringe-making and would often be met by a choreography of eye-rolling from all their children. I'd have to say that they very much enjoyed our embarrassment, a feeling I now inflict on my own children.

I can still remember how mortifying I thought it all was, particularly if I had any of those pale, perfect, skinny Australian girls around. The parents of my Anglo friends did not behave like that in public, whereas the appetites of my family were manifest in our bodies. Large, loud, enthusiastic.

But all the cringing stopped when I became interested in sex myself. Which was around the age of twelve.

Did I grow up too fast because my parents were public about their sexuality? My mind grew up about the same time as my body, which started to sprout when I was about ten. By eleven, I had breasts that were leaning away from my body. And twenty days after my twelfth birthday, I had my first period.

You know that story you hear about mothers getting excited about the onset of a daughter's periods? Yep. That was my mother. It elicited the same enthusiastic response as when, much later, I came first in my Ancient History trials in what we now call Year 11. I really have no idea how to piece these two responses together unless I imagine that what she observed was all the desirable traits of a young woman coming together. Brains. Fertility. What else could possibly matter?

And yes, I lost my virginity not long after I hit puberty. I rarely talk about it because most people are scandalised that I was so young. *Surely you were taken advantage of. Surely you didn't know what you were doing.*

But that is a gross underestimation of the kind of girl I was – and the kind of woman I am. I knew exactly what I wanted and who I wanted and set out to have those things. At twelve. It wasn't exactly how my mother described intercourse, but I thought it was probably a little bit like doing your times tables: the more you did it, the better you would get at it. (This comparison may appear a little glib to you, but the fact is my mother made it clear that women enjoyed sex. She did. I would. I was a woman, I was unafraid, and would therefore enjoy sex.)

I write this brief history only to make it possible for you to see how I've arrived at thirty-seven years of sex with one man. And to still be enjoying it.

There have, of course, been gaps. Particularly in my vagina, wrenched asunder by giant babies. But a little more of that later.

Yes, thanks to my parents, I've always had this model of what good sex is: two people making each other feel good and eventually having an orgasm in one way or another. This apparently makes me lucky, say my non-orgasmic female friends. But it is what I expected and what I still have.

Friends and even acquaintances will occasionally ask questions. One friend, with a hunger for both sex and novelty, asks me how I can bear having sex with the same person for such a long time. Which completely misunderstands the human condition, or at least my human condition.

I am not still having sex with the same person. We've both changed so many times. So many.

We met when we were children, or at least twenty-two and twenty-four. It didn't take us all that long to start having the kind of sex you have when you are that age – pleasure arrives like an uncontrolled hose, all twists and spurts, desire (very briefly) pent up and then spent. Whoosh.

And if that's the only kind of sex you've ever encountered – if, for instance, all the sex you've ever had is with people who've requited your instant unknowing lust – that's what it's probably been like all your life. A shag, an orgasm and a nap. On to the next. There is no need to negotiate beyond your next orgasm because that's the end game.

But once you spend nights together, and nights end on end when you've worked all day, sex becomes more than the uncontrolled hose. It has to if you want your sex life to survive. Of course, it's still about desire but that desire is tempered by work hours; work days, work nights. It's also about learning to negotiate, learning to wait, learning to hold on.

It is also coming to an understanding that it's not bed-trembling every single time. Not bed-trembling and not epic. Your partner is tired. You are tired. You've had too much to eat or to drink.

And sex must make room for the rest of life. Annoying but true. It's absolutely not possible – or at least it wasn't for me – to feel instantly aroused after a twelve-hour day in a newsroom. More often, my brain would be utterly preoccupied with whatever horror to which police rounds had exposed me.

So, two sets of people so far. The breathless lusty types without a care in the world, having sex whenever, wherever.

I would specify some of the more public locations but I'm shy. The newly bejobbed, both intensely focused on new careers but trying to ensure our relationship and our sex life survived. There was a lot of planning for weekend camping trips, where it was possible to decompress. Oh god, I loved those weekends away. I even overcame my fear of sleeping outdoors because of the sheer pleasure of sex under stars and moon.

By our second wedding anniversary, however, I was six months pregnant. Those are the people we became next. Parents.

Challenges and opportunities. So many challenges; and the more kids you have, the fewer opportunities. We had three children. Still, lots of desire – or at least longing – but our kids shared our bed, which made sex tricky. Neither pregnancy nor childbirth did much to dampen my libido – strangely, with our third, my desire was completely out of control. I can't even share what happened to me during this time because some of it even makes me blush.

When you have three kids under five and two full-time jobs, exhaustion takes over your body and the children take over your bed. No privacy, no energy, no space, no time. But sex was a way we kept close, even if it meant having sex in the bathroom or the dining room while the kids snuffled in our bed. We kept having sex. We also kept talking. These two activities kept us connected even as our friends' relationships fell apart around us. We kept having sex because we liked it. It helped to keep us close. Talking is good and crucial, but touching makes a difference.

I remember our first weekend away, when our eldest was a young teenager. We stayed at a friend's house while they were away. We were unashamedly and unabashedly noisy and it was so much fun. That was a hint of what was to come, later, later.

There are stages you expect in your married life if you are as conventional as me. And then there is the unexpected – sickness, death.

About twenty-five years into our marriage, my sister died; and a few months later, still gripped by fear and sorrow and feeling so bleak, I discovered my GP had given me such bad advice about the results of my pap smear. I had what the gynaecologist called an emergency hysterectomy.

You get a few choices when you are having one of those surgeries, and I decided to keep my ovaries. I had a few older friends who told me that when they lost their ovaries, they lost their sex drives. Others who'd had sudden-onset menopause found that their vaginas dried up, became scratchy, inconsolable. If I'd known better and had more time to do research, I would have recognised that menopause is nearly as unique to each woman as fingerprints. Still, I did decide to keep my ovaries. They are inside me, shrivelling slowly.

So began the slow descent into menopause, when my libido was meant to disappear. Why didn't it?

I have a few theories. There is so much loveliness in having kids but there is no doubt that it's also scary and occasionally a burden. If your marriage survives all that, you are still with the person you love and desire. It's also true that, if your marriage survives that long, those adorable burdens leave home. You have more disposable income, you feel more free. That research which says the more money you earn, the more sex you have? It turns out to be true. Not because money makes you sexier, or your partner sexier, but because you finally stop worrying. Nothing stops an orgasm quicker than worrying about whether you can pay the childcare fees next week.

Women are not meant to feel like this. If I wanted role models for how I would feel when my kids left home, those role models would teach me to be sad, to feel as if I'd lost something. But truly, I felt proud. They were adults with adult relationships, they had friends and jobs and education.

And all of that made me feel more confident and powerful, more within myself. When I read the Relationships Australia research which said that there was an increase in the number of people aged seventy and over who were very satisfied with their sex lives, I totally got that. It wasn't as if that group of people were suddenly as erect or tumescent as they had been in their thirties, but the other things which also make sex good, they were better. Our environment. Our capacity to buy beds that prevent bad backs while still trying to maintain youthful agility. That same research said that once we hit forty, we start to enjoy sex again. Except for those who are having their first babies at forty (okay, I made that bit up).

I once wrote that nothing has the same aphrodisiac qualities as a) the kids leaving home, and b) having more money because those same young people have left home.

When they left home, we started to go out together again, we started to travel, we made the time for each other just as we had right at the beginning. But there was something else happening to me that I didn't fully understand despite a deep and abiding interest in the health of my vagina and its surrounds.

I was starting to feel like my vagina and I were losing it. Contact with my beloved's penis did not feel the same to me. I'd been doing those demanding pelvic-floor exercises like a champion, many times a day. I'd always prided myself on having the kind of pelvic control that meant I could stop peeing midway and not leak.

But something weird was happening and, when I started to put together the life history of my brilliant vagina, I realised the changes had started soon after delivering a 4.66-kilogram baby in ninety minutes.

Vaginal childbirth gets the worst press. But to me, it's quite an orgasmic feeling, delivering a baby. This powerful tiny being squirms its way out, much like a big fish swimming down a small stream. The kind of urgent, pounding contractions I have during orgasm. I've written before about how impressed I was with my vagina but, truly, I felt confident it could do anything.

What it didn't seem to be able to do, however, was to pull itself back together, no matter what I did about it. One of the changes I didn't love was the fact that the whoomp of the contractions of my orgasm wasn't feeling the same way it used to. In fact, I could barely feel that pulsing at all. I started to investigate a vaginal reconstruction secretly but when you mention that to friends they immediately accuse your partner of complaining.

But for me, it was me. I was complaining. I wanted my old vagina back and with it my old orgasms.

It was just by accident that I mentioned this to the woman who would perform my hysterectomy. We were both watching a video of what would happen during my surgery when I admired the vagina of the woman in the clip. The gynie asked me some questions, and within one consultation we'd both decided that a vaginal reconstruction would be a very good idea.

She couldn't explain why all my exercises and all my Pilates hadn't put my vagina back together again but I really felt great trust in her. I was less sure about my friends – people get very judgey about elective surgery – but it didn't feel elective to me. I love penetrative sex and wanted to continue to get pleasure out of it.

The gynaecologist and I had quite a few conversations about what kind of vagina I wanted, and the truth is I didn't need the vagina of a twenty-year-old woman. After all, I wasn't planning to have sex with a twenty-year-old man. Not everything needed to be as it was in its original packaging – pert, plump and perfectly formed. I just wanted it to be fit for purpose, which, at my age, was not about delivering gigantic babies.

And people! It works in just the way I wanted it to work. My orgasms feel buzzy and strong. Much like me. (Joke.)

Oh. Blushing now. That was all some revelation. I know older women aren't meant to talk about the joy of sex, much less experience it. We are meant to pretend that as our hair goes grey, so does our desire, as if it leaches out of us; that as our ovaries wither, so should our libidos. Sex is for the young and perky. Well, sisters, I have news for you.

It turns out that my parents gave me the capacity to do more than just enjoy sex. They also gave me some ability to nurture the relationship inside which my sex life bloomed, and – body, brain and relationship willing – still does.

Now we are different people again.

Older. Much older. Between us, every day, there is some small twinge somewhere. Lower back. Maybe the odd knee. We do more exercise than we ever did in our twenties yet we also feel it more. We are no longer endlessly taut; well, not every day anyway, and that brings new sensations too. We are even more tender with each other than we were before and our skins fold together.

The chatting hasn't changed much. So much chat. We talk, we interrupt each other, we listen, we grumble, we listen some more. It turns out that all the touching in the world will only work if you also do all the talking in the world.

YOU KNOW WHAT ANNOYS ME ABOUT
ROM-COM MOVIE SEX? YOU NEVER SEE
THE GIRL PEEING FURIOUSLY AFTERWARDS
AND SCULLING CRANBERRY JUICE IN
A BID TO AVOID A UTI.

FUCK THE MEET-CUTE

MARIA LEWIS

Meet-cute: a situation or occasion when potential romantic partners meet for the first time in a charming or amusing way: a classic Hollywood meet-cute; his meet-cute with Jane in the bookstore.[1]

'Listen, I just wanted to say you're really beautiful and seem really interesting. I'd love to get to know you.' Those were the first words out of his mouth and usually, *usually*, they would have had me making a dismissive wanking gesture into thin air. Yet I had watched with curiosity as the tallest man I had ever seen in real-D crossed two lanes of traffic to come up and speak to me. I'm barely five foot six and, although this gent looked tall from a distance, as he drew closer I found myself leaning back to digest his full height of six foot eleven.

'Um ...' I replied, ever literate.

'I know people don't usually do this,' he quickly added, blushing as he ran a hand through his ginger hair nervously.

'Well, no, they don't, and kudos to you. You must have serious balls.'

This was not my usual interaction with strange men on the street. At most, I'd get a 'NICE TITS, PURPLE!' as they leant out of the passenger side of their best friend's Daewoo, and I would choose to either a) flip the bird or b) screech 'YOU'RE AN EMBARRASSMENT TO THE WOMEN IN YOUR LIFE' as they accelerated off into the distance. Conversely, I might spot a cute guy and make wavering eye contact before deciding they probably liked Michael Bay movies and writing them off. This man, though, he was sweet. Daggy, bespectacled and respectful: all cursory ticks. And he had wandered into my life during a period when I was feeling adventurous, free-spirited and open to the world. Not open to love, mind you. I always had a clear and present thought that I would avoid love – and commitment, and attachment, and *feelings* – as best I could, since I had watched with voyeuristic interest what those things had done to my friends. The pain? Didn't seem worth it. Fun experiences with new and interesting people? I'm someone who can happily go months without wanting to engage with anyone outside of my inner circle and the thought of even flirting with the opposite sex tires me. Yet I was coming out of one such slump and feeling … interested.

We exchanged numbers and agreed to meet up the next day after work. In the less than twenty-four hours that passed, I did what I always did when I was interested in someone and wanted to remain unmurdered: I entered their name into every possible database I had access to. Given that I've been a journalist for over a decade, suffice to say that's quite a few. I had guided many girl and boy friends away from potential icebergs by first searching for the object of their affection in said databases, and it had never led us astray before. This guy, I saw, came up relatively clean. No convictions, no hidden wife, no secretly racist Tumblr page. And I say relatively clean because there were two things: just minor ones. He was listed as being in an 'open relationship' on Facebook and so was his partner. No big. Also, he had kinda, maybe, sorta caused a stir by chaining himself to a train to protest a mining project.

Huh, I thought, as I clicked through the picture archives, looking at the incident from twelve months earlier. His personal politics were a sharper branch of my own – it wasn't like I had found him protesting out the front of an abortion clinic or something malicious.

Well, at least he's passionate about something, I reasoned, trying to imagine what could drive me to the same situation. Maybe if they cancelled *New 52 Batman* I'd be driven to protest too.

I cast any niggling doubts aside and met him for our 'date'. Generally speaking, I hate dates: it's all the same bullshit with people reading off their résumés and adding phrases like 'one day I'd like to travel to' and 'my ultimate dream would be'. Horseshit. They all hit the same beats and are mostly boring as fuck. Yet I pushed through with this, answering all the inane questions and pretending to be interested in his stories. Why? Largely because I wanted to open myself up to new people – new possibilities – and I was intrigued by the idea of sleeping with someone who was six foot eleven. That had never been on my sexual bucket list until our fatuous meet-cute, yet now it was not only inked on there but also within reach.

If he sensed my boredom he didn't mention it, but he did readily agree when I suggested we go back to his place a few hours later. I texted a friend his address on the sly, just in case he turned out to be a Michael Fassbender, and I was weirdly mystified when we reached his address in a trendy suburb next to my own. His house made The Burrow look like a mansion, with there being such a blatant disregard for amenities that the bathroom was lacking a sink – it had only a bowl with water in it instead. My thinly veiled horror upon returning from the loo was momentarily forgotten as I caught a glimpse of the lounge. Every spare space of wall was lined with comic books. Not collected volumes, mind you. There were hundreds of trade issues, bagged and boarded like a true believer.

Finally, I thought. *Something to be attracted to. Let's use this.*

The comics, however, did not belong to The Guy. They were the lifelong collection of his roommate: a transgender woman who swept into the room wrapped in a white, see-through robe with a faux fur trim. It was glorious. She introduced herself as 'Sweetheart' and I immediately envisaged us becoming best friends who solved crimes in urban Sydney. She had recently sold half her collection, she informed me, to pay for her cat's surgery after he was hit by a car. Unfortunately Sweetheart didn't stay long, sensing an invisible cue from The Guy, and she sashayed out of the room with more grace than Jones. I longed for her to stay, to keep talking with me about comics, yet slowly the conversation moved into the bedroom, where I was at first delighted to see *Star Wars* sheets on his bed and then horrified to see they were vintage *Star Wars* sheets kept from childhood. There's nothing that makes your vagina seal itself shut quicker than a grown-arse man still sleeping in the linen from his youth.

fast forward twenty minutes

Reader, I slept with him. I'd like to say I had more dignity or, heck, even standards. But when you wanna get laid, you wanna get laid. And it was terrible. So terrible, in fact, that I texted a friend 'SEX SOS' two minutes post-coitus and – knowing the drill – she called me immediately. Getting dressed as casually as I could, I had a one-sided conversation with an imaginary flatmate who was locked out of our sharehouse and 'desperately' needed me to come and let her in.

'Right now? I mean, yeah, I could come and let you in,' I sighed, giving The Guy a look of annoyance.

'You had gross heterosexual sex, didn't you? Men are gross,' said my friend on the other end.

'No no, if you gotta get in you gotta get in,' I replied.

'Can you see his penis right now? No, don't tell me. I'll throw up.'

'Uh-huh, it's fine. I owe you a favour. I'll see you in twenty.'

'You should burn your clothes.'

'Bye.'

I explained to my still-naked and limp-dicked counter-part that I had to go, with there simply being no other option for it given my third flatmate was 'out of the country'.

He asked if I wanted to stay for dinner. I said that I didn't. He asked if I had to leave. I said that I did. He asked if we could do this again sometime. I said probably not.

He took my hasty exit calmly, trying to keep up the small talk and not to look offended when I dodged his kiss at the front door like Neo would bullets in *The Matrix*. When I had power-walked down the block and as far away from his lair of sexual disappointment as I could, I did my best not to break out into a run.

I had barely been gone ten minutes when my phone buzzed in my jeans pocket and I glanced down to see his name flashing across the screen. I groaned, but answered.

'Hiya,' I said, the exasperation audible in my voice.

'Hey, it's me.'

'Yup, I know.'

'I just wanted to see if you were okay—'

'Well, I mean the sex wasn't great but emotionally I'm fine,' I replied, anticipating his question.

There was a long pause on the other end of the line before he continued.

'Ah, no, I mean because just after you left the cops came by. Apparently someone got stabbed next door?'

'Oh … *oh*. Uh, well, it wasn't me.'

'Okay. Right. Have a good night, I guess.'

'You too, bye!'

I cringed as I hung up, but my momentary guilt over his potential hurt feelings was replaced with the relief of not being in his company anymore. I returned home to a house full of flatmates and was able to decompress as I relived the past few hours' worth of anecdotes over a cup of tea and half a pack of Tim Tams. Okay, okay: a *whole* packet of Tim Tams.

'What the fuck were you thinking?' one flatmate asked.

'Well, I thought it was really ballsy to approach someone on the street like that – not knowing anything about them – and tell them how you felt,' I offered.

'It's like something out of a movie,' my other flatmate said, before adding, 'except for the disappointing ending.'

'You know what annoys me about rom-com movie sex? You never see the girl peeing furiously afterwards and sculling cranberry juice in a bid to avoid a UTI,' I said.

'Journalists,' my first flatmate groaned, answering the question in my raised eyebrows. 'You essentially went on a date with this guy – shagged him – because it sounded like the beginning of a good story.'

I pondered that before deciding that, yeah, it was true. So few of my romantic liaisons – whether a one-night stand or someone I had properly dated – had ever started with a cool story. They just kinda, always, happened. I wanted that Year One level of awesome origin story, yet in reality what had that gotten me? Not an orgasm. Romantic notions of the meet-cute had led me down a path I was usually quite reluctant to tread and I was peeved about it. I had a thought that this might be one of those gateway patriarchy drugs, so stealthy and insidious that they slide into your life and redefine your expectations before you have a chance to call bullshit or actively decide that this is what you do or do not want. Much in the same way, babes I'd known to never care much for weddings suddenly became obsessed with floral arrangements – the colour schemes – the seating plans – as they planned their own big day, only to ask months down the track, *What the fuck happened to me?* The examples of it were endless: women being subliminally coaxed into fulfilling gender roles because that's what they were *supposed* to do at one point or another. Had I fallen for the same trick? Had I sipped from the fictional romantic Kool-Aid – the recipe of which had been cooked up by a handful of cis white males in a Hollywood writers' room?

A good night's sleep worked as a beautiful reset button for my thoughts, and I started the next day with only the vaguest emotional hangover. By mid-morning I was so deeply immersed in work that the previous night's events had been erased from my mind. That is, until my phone's message tone pinged in my bag and I saw a message from The Guy flash across my screen. It read: 'Can't wait to peel off your Wonder Woman panties and lick your cunt.'

I threw my phone in the trash. I considered grabbing a packet of matches and igniting the bin, just to be safe. Never in my life had I been so turned off by something intended to turn me on. First of all, it was 11.38 am. On a Wednesday. That is not an a-fucking-m message. That is not a pre-lunch message. That is a post-11.00 pm message on a Friday night, if at all. Secondly, peel? PEEL? My vagina is not a banana. Thirdly, cunt – while being one of my favourite words and unfairly blacklisted in society – is not something you get to call *my* vagina after just one meeting with it. Lady Vagina Jacaranda the Third would suffice. Or Miss Vagina Dentata. But cunt? I cut The Guy off quicker than a snake-bitten limb. Gone and blocked from my phone he was. Friend requests on Facebook would be forever ignored. I tore up my sexual bucket list and tossed out my Wonder Woman panties. It was no never mind: I had another six pairs waiting in the wings. If there was a lesson here, I said to myself, it was this: never again give in to the meet-cute. Fuck the meet-cute – but never literally.

WHEN A KISS IS THE PRIZE FOR
GOOD CONVERSATION, IT'S IMPRESSIVE
HOW MUCH CONVERSATIONS IMPROVE.

THE PRIZE FOR
GOoD CONVERSATION

VAN BADHAM

The first time I ever french-kissed someone, I was fifteen and at a backyard party in Earlwood, one of Sydney's suburbs.

It was the early 1990s. I remember there were coloured lightbulbs hanging off a wooden fence for decoration. Someone's cousin was the DJ and commercial R&B was blaring – Salt-N-Pepa, Black Box – and the crowded yard was heaving with local kids. I didn't like the music and I didn't know the guests but the host was my friend Helen, and despite being her arty-weirdo friend from a school a few suburbs away from Earlwood and a neighbourhood even further than that, I'd made an effort to fit in. I'd brushed my hair for the first time in months. I'd restrained from caking my eyes with drawn experiments in black eyeliner. I was wearing a short red dress, bought at a department-store summer sale, and I danced to the music even though

I'd been listening to The Velvet Underground and David Bowie alone in my room for two years.

I don't know how I got talking to Nicky, who was also fifteen and Greek-Australian like Helen. I don't remember what he said, or how he convinced me to take a walk with him away from the house, down the quiet street, and towards a shadowy street-side power box where he pressed himself into the modest darkness and, with it, me.

Then, his warm tongue and lips were on mine, his hands were on my shoulders, my back was pressed against the cool metal of the power box. My body softened at his first touch – inspired, ignited.

I was an only child, a loner and a student at a single-sex school, and my only understanding of sex was theoretical – movies, books, TV and magazines had arranged sex in my mind as some kind of limb-bound, mouth-borne wrestle. I was unprepared for the delightful wetness and heat of his mouth, the instant sweat on my limbs, the furious acceleration of contact that was causing my cunt to moisten and ache. The faster his tongue moved, the tighter I wanted to hold him. It was I who placed his hands on my breasts, then guided his fingers under my bra-strap and into the soft pocket between the bra-cup and my flesh. With each of his squeezes, my desire ballooned – *yes*, I said, as he dropped his face into my naked breasts, kissed and sucked. *Yes*, I said, as his fingers went under my dress and felt for my thighs, for the edge of my pants, for the lips of my gushing cunt. I shifted my hips to admit his fingertips to the unexplored landscape inside me and – delighted, discovered – I shifted again, enveloping each grasping fingerbone to his knuckle.

If he was talking, I wasn't listening; my every thought fixated on my electrified wet flesh wrenching open or the hard mystery I felt at his crotch – grinding, sliding and stabbing. I burned at the wonderful anger of hands snatching fabric, the mutual shoving of muscle and bone. He pulled my hair and I gave a joyous, breathless yelp.

Ah, Nicky – if Helen hadn't come looking for me, her voice somehow sounding my name over the wet smacking of all our lips and kisses, I would have fucked you there. And hard.

I told Helen she could give Nicky my number. He called me a few times, but – too soon – I became oblique in our conversations, indirect in my responses, uninterested in his questions. I was far more fascinated by the sudden awareness of my own sexuality than with the random boy who'd unleashed it.

What I discovered was that my liberation from inexperience was something perceptible by sight – perhaps even by scent – and a tasting plate of delicious teen adventure was being offered to me. The appeal of Nicky faded as I felt myself attuned to a broader sexual current of glances and gestures and the temperature of space that certain bodies could heat. A boy called Adam sought me out on the crowded deck of a boat. One named Dave lured me away from a beach gathering into spinifex and sand dunes. Mike stole me away from a party into an erotic lightlessness found behind a lockable bathroom door. There were others in less memorable locations, yet I absorbed – and probably even now retain – the energy generated by those events of attraction, desire and wet ignition. I fed on furtive kisses, rough hands and saliva, the give of limbs, the oral explorations of cocks and cunts, learning, from boy to boy and mouth to mouth, the nuances of their pleasures and my own.

And yet, despite great curiosity and yearning, naked revelations and contortions of the spine, I didn't 'fuck' these boys. The only foolish mistake I made amid these activities was admit to all their details while bragging to my friends. My small girl-gang was, of course, engaged in the exact same explorations with their own boy admirers – and yet, among us all, a curious mania for policing the act of penetration-by-penis took hold. We were all now sixteen, sexually awake and thoroughly cock-addled, yet culture mounts an effective invasion of the brain. Fairytales masquerading as learned advice in magazines and folk tales instructed us that good girls waited and first times were supposed to be 'special'; a heterosexual girl's 'devirgination' without romantic love pre-pledged was some kind of irrecoverable female failure.

These days I think back on this nonsense with furious horror, now aware to the mitochondria in each of my cells that 'sex' is an experience defined by the mutual realisation of intimate contact, not the geolocation of a cock. But I'm encumbered by my past, and still use the word 'fuck' as straight-girl, shorthand slang for a specific act of penetrative copulation – others, of course, have and deserve their own definitions. When I was sixteen, the question 'Did you fuck him?' meant only one thing, and at the time it had the connotation of some kind of surrender – a giving up or giving in – as if the act of true sexual completion was relenting your physical territory to male occupation. We had already enjoyed boys' tongues in our hungriest corners, we'd learnt how to make them come with our hands, we'd seen pearly jizz, vulnerability and nakedness, tried out spaces and places, and even toyed at the edges of fetish with blindfolds, candlewax and ice cubes ... And yet in the tangible presence of cock we felt obliged to remain lock-kneed – despite all personal instinct to the precise opposite.

Perhaps in generations before contraceptives, prophylactics and abortion rights, such sexual reticence was sensible. But my friends and I were children of the AIDS wave, with condoms on sale at every chemist and given out free on World AIDS Day. For all my conditional puritanism, I carried two of these in my wallet – copper-coloured wrappers, emblazoned with stars, a gift from a friend – and I bristled with burning disinclination to piety. Aloud, I made out my intentions were those of a 'good girl' and declared that I wanted a boyfriend – my girl-gang joked I wanted everyone else's. The reality was

I was restless and weird, the kind of teenager cursed with no ability to pretend I was anything but a teenager, and my attention span barely stretched to the edges of myself, let alone into any territory of truly wanting to pair.

To teach myself who I was, I engaged in experiments with behaviour and persona, from arty loner to screaming rebel to terrified nerd to wild slut in all the costumes each character demanded. Underneath the performance, my body craved to fuck boys with worshipful fury, convenience and detachment. A generation before, feminist Erica Jong had named the object of such yearning a 'zipless fuck', but I had no words, literature or lived experience to identify such things, or to realise I was not alone in this craving. Good girls waited. The first time had to be special. Love was important. I pinned romantic aspirations on the human subjects of my sexual fantasies because I did not want to feel shame.

Then, I discovered alcohol.

The first time I ever had penetrative sex with someone, I was seventeen and at a backyard party in Miranda, one of Sydney's suburbs.

It was the early 1990s. I don't remember the decorations, because I was drunk. I don't remember the music, because I was drunk. I sort of remember that the crowded yard was heaving with local kids and I was drinking either Blue Vok or Midori from a plastic cup, mixed with lemonade … or maybe I was necking it from the bottle straight. I'd been kicked out of my single-sex state school in one suburb and had arrived at a co-ed one several suburbs away, and now I drank because the kids here all did and I didn't know how else to fit in.

Who the hell knows what I was wearing, or what I'd been blabbering all night. Some hazy recollection involves me kissing my friend Peter, maybe – maybe my friend Daniel, too. I think my friend Abigail tried to get me to leave and maybe I hollered at her, but as this took place in the days before smartphones, there is no SMS trail or Facebook photo record to determine the events of the evening.

I don't know how I got talking to Ciaran. I can't remember whether he was seventeen, eighteen or even nineteen, what he looked like or even what he was doing at my friend Mischa's eighteenth-birthday party. I have no recollection what he said, or how he convinced me to take a walk with him away from the crowd, to the front lawn of the house. I don't even remember making out with him.

I do remember that I lay on my back on the ground, and I felt twigs stick in the back of my skull, and that someone – maybe him, maybe me – pulled down my underpants. One of us extricated his cock from his unzipped fly and rolled a condom over it, and then, with none of the heat, passion, sweat, desire or enthusiasm that had opened me so readily to Nicky or the other boys, he lay on top of me and the fucking happened.

My body was so numbed with booze that what I felt was mostly cold curiosity while distant, uncomfortable thrusting and buckling took place. The only other sensation swimming in my mind was a blurry relief that I was, at last, unburdened of the virginity I'd worn like an iron collar. When Ciaran came, I checked out – the next thing I knew, it was dull, white morning. Somehow, I was awake on the floor of Mischa's bedroom. She slept in a bunk bed. I had a desperate urge for a shower.

Once in the bathroom, it took some seconds under the water for my bruised, hungover body to process the events of the night before. There was a little blood between my legs. I pulled some twigs out of my hair. Suds washed over me, and I reflected that, while my body ached now, the act itself had not been painful.

It was coincidence that I then slumped against the shower wall, and burst into tears.

Sexual consciousness is the internal map you create to navigate the nature of your own desire. At seventeen, I didn't have it. I was young and had been so inculcated with sexual shame that the only permission I could provide myself for wanting to fuck without emotional commitment was the pretext of being very drunk. I stayed drunk for another seventeen years.

If I have one regret in life, it's every alcoholic drink I've ever had. I drank a lot and too often, for too long. I just got too used to applying booze to numb a shame I didn't deserve, but couldn't manage to shift.

This is supposed to be a happy story about 'doing it'; I

promise I didn't spend the next near-two-decades unloved or sexually miserable. A couple of lacklustre boys after Ciaran, I won my dreamt-of zipless fuck from a pretty punk I picked up at a party. From memory there was a long bus ride home, and perhaps due to some sobering up on the journey and the delicious restraint of the bus, we stumbled into my room and collapsed with a sweaty alacrity for kissing, fucking and being nude. Although half-drunk, my body remembered this energy; we had sex again and again until we burned up the end of the night into a cool and smouldering grey morning. When I woke up, my hair stank like his tongue. I wrapped myself in sticky sheets and he rode his skateboard off in the direction of Never Again. I waved and smiled.

Soon enough, I was at university, and only barely more mature. To win a drunken twenty-dollar bet with my flatmate, I elected myself to deflower the shy boy from downstairs. At the party, I talked him into more drinks and we kissed to Nirvana's 'Smells like Teen Spirit'. He was shaking as I led him to my room. In the morning, I left him in my bed with some hazy exit instructions and took off for a weekend in Sydney. Imagine my surprise when I returned two days later and found him still there. His politeness was to sit in front of the door, not behind it, and to ask if we were together. I said yes, and let myself love him. He was kind and good. We dated for over a year. I liked the regular sex, and I wasn't always drunk when we did it. I was just drunk for most of the time.

And not just drunk – a drunk. My drunk persona was a wild mess, as inclined to a pub-wide shouting match as weeping around a party's corners or a frenzied pash-up in a cab. A certain kind of boy who liked a drink liked a drunk who arrived to drink already half drunk under the table. My inebriation indulged wannabe rockstars, young communists, buttoned-up nerds and ex-cons in their desires for unrestrained madness. The problem was when they reached for the mad girl the next day, they grasped only the thin arm of the quivering hangover that had replaced her. I coined the term 'awareness sickness' for the heavy, painful revelations that beset the mornings after one-night stands, and I fled many scenes in a nausea of panicked regret. The relationships that summoned themselves from liquid-chemical beginnings were just as fraught: how could I believe that those attracted to the drunk persona would be satisfied with me, who was so much smaller, shy and lacking the brass of the girl who'd slammed down those shots at the bar? So I played the drunk even when the drinking was over. Inside, I was the worm that languished in an empty bottle when the tequila was long finished.

It was a bottle this worm had outgrown. By thirty-four, the hangovers were dangerous, my self-anxiety was exhausted and my attention span was thin; I'd grown bored with sloppy hookups after the greasy nights in bars, and tired of relationships that were one-third lies, one-third sex, one-third shouting. I was in London now, and a drunken transcontinental phone call ended the drunken relationship I'd had with the boy far too young for me who'd replaced another drinking boy before that happened and some drunk ones from earlier on. The next morning, I was flooded with an awareness sickness that seemed terminal. My guts burned as my mind replayed every scene of regret it had the details to remember, and when a few days later I tried a sip of wine, the poison churned against the rotten cells of my stomach with such viciousness that I have not had a drink since.

I have had dates, though, and kisses. And, unforeseen miracle, I've had sex, too. To my surprise, the first awkward, post-sobriety kiss was all the more erotic for being so. Drunk seductions are a clumsy tactility of bold gambits at pawing. They pale in comparison to sobriety's second-by-second courtship diplomacy – of irises, eyelashes, head tilts and hip twists – and the escalations of flirting. When a kiss is the prize for good conversation, it's impressive how much conversations improve. It's impressive, too, how attuned you become to attraction's other, silent communications, and how well you can then calibrate a flirtation. There are subtle scents that booze can drown, and mechanics of muscle and bone whose rough operation sobriety smoothens. Narcissism, thuggery, meanness and cruelty can lie buried in another's character; booze can excuse them, but deliberate soberness rings out sharp alarms.

So what I learnt 'doing it' sober was that, by virtue of drinking at all, I'd spent years 'doing it' wrong. Now I'd dropped the personas, pretexts and the chemical masks, in the act of sex I was finally naked – and desired, on my own terms, for the first time.

And how does that feel? It's fucking great, and vice versa. It's the sex I should have had at fifteen, mouth full of tongue in the shadows of that power box with Nicky, ignoring the call of my friend when she came to look for me. It's the sex I should have let myself have among the lips and limbs of so many perfect, sticky boys in those lost teenage years of summer, whose sensations I remember, but whose days I can't clutch back.

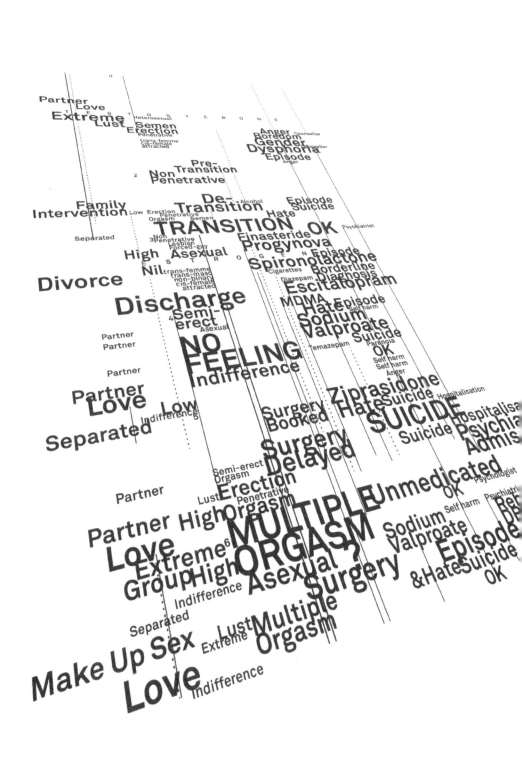

TRANSITIONING MEDICATED BORDERLINERS DO IT EXTREMELY – IF AT ALL

SIMONA CASTRICUM

My relationship with sex has always been somewhat problematic and charged with confusion, chaos and compromise. My transition presented a chance to find some comfort and some peace with my identity, my body and my sexual energy. It was time to stop living vicariously through other people and step into the unknown, a departure from the devil I knew I wanted nothing more to do with, the devil that I had fooled myself to accept.

This diagram maps the emotional and pharmaceutical context around three major events: TRANSITION, NO FEELING and MULTIPLE ORGASM. I've tried to map my experience of gender transition since first deciding it was time to treat my apparent gender dysphoria – something I had lived through in various guises since childhood. It records a six-year journey of sexual confusion, turmoil and triumph. The text size represents the intensity and significance of emotions, experiences and events. Broken lines indicate fractured and latent conditions, while solid lines articulate constant linkages and certain states. In isolation and up close these emotions and events have an obvious relationship; however, the diagram is deliberately chaotic and confusing – perhaps even impossible to understand – because that is what it's like for me. So if you're lost, I don't blame you. I am too, most – if not all – of the time.

We can all relate to the idea that our sexual energy is connected with our wider wellbeing and personal circumstance. But what makes medical gender transition unique is the way it changes a person's hormonal conditions. It's changed my sexual energy in profound and beautiful ways; I understand my body's capacity for pleasure in better ways than I did before. Before I transitioned, I knew that result-focused thrusting and gendered, penetrative fucking was one way to experience eroticism, but not my idea of a good time. Transition has enabled me to be present in sex where activities are more diverse and about partnership. Sex is more sensual, contemplative, negotiated, instinctive. It's longer – much longer, yet slower and softer – then harder, faster, again and again. Sex has become exploratory; it has more space to feel.

Meanwhile I enjoy a changed body. My skin and muscles are softer, my smell is salty, my hair is finer. My nipples and my breasts are perfect simply because they exist. My body is beautiful – it looks and feels the way I have always felt it should be, a femininity I enjoy and celebrate. Understanding my genitals again has been the biggest challenge. Just sitting with the notion that I will still have a penis for the immediate future is something I've had to adjust to. Not all transgender women undergo surgery. In my experience, the expense and recovery process are in themselves prohibitive; the surgery requires a lot of support and mental toughness to endure. I've been scheduled for the operation twice and have had to postpone it for both psychological and financial reasons. It seems like something so unattainable that to focus on it will only hold me back from the work ahead of me in the short term. And even if it never happens, so what? Coming to the conclusion that my genitalia don't determine my gender has been a process for me.

Meanwhile, I've developed a much better relationship with my penis, scrotum and perineum through their feminine energy. Knowing how these areas of skin respond under oestrogen and what areas might one day form my labia, clitoris and vaginal opening has redefined masturbation and sex for me. Best thing of all is I come harder and for longer periods of time, and there are about three or four ways the sensation can pass through my body – depending on how I'm experiencing it and who with. The boring drill of grunt, thrust and ejaculation of semen has been replaced by a more graceful shaking, blissful moaning and erotic convulsions with a negligible sticky discharge.

I experience orgasm with the joyous hands-in-the-air screaming dance of a woman on MDMA on top of my partner's shoulders at a festival – not a bad place to transcend to. My partner is a big part of being able to find confidence in my body and it's a discovery we've been able to share that's quite unique.

But it took some time to get here – and this wonderful space is something that I've experienced with limited consistency. Transition has moved me into challenging and alienating spaces – in bed, in my heart and in my head. This change is further compounded by lived experiences of exclusion, abuse, ridicule and victimisation. Real and imagined abandonment, feelings of undesirability, and being rejected purely because I am transgender: all these things cut deep inside.

To experience gender dysphoria, to come out as transgender and to transition can expose us to significant mental illness. An alarming number of transwomen live medicated lives to manage unique presentations of depression, anxiety and stress triggered by trauma and loss.

Borderline Personality Disorder (BPD) is not an uncommon added complexity to gender dysphoria, and I need a cocktail of antidepressants and antipsychotics to help me manage. Anybody who lives a medicated existence will understand how it affects sexual energy. That not only has implications for our own bodies but can also have adverse effects on our relationships – the way we interact with each other through sex becomes compromised. One of BPD's qualities is the extreme experience of emotions and the propensity to indulge recklessly in vices, through which we seek escape. I'm only just coming to understand how connected sex is to my mental health. My sexual energy switches between extreme states of hypersexuality, where I'm trying to break a world record in eroticism, and asexuality, where I'm totally uninterested in it. What is curious is that under oestrogen I'm mostly sexually passive – under testosterone I felt constantly hypersexual.

The last six months have given me a lot of hope and my partner and I enjoy this. The bottom left-hand corner of the diagram marks 'multiple orgasms, love' – I'll take more of that, please. I hope for something less chaotic and a triumphant path through undesirability, over-medication and surgery. While the volatile borderline between illness and transition remains one to navigate with care, the rebuilding of my sexual identity continues with some optimism and freedom in its uncertainty, spontaneity and adventure.

IN RETROSPECT, SEX WORK
WAS NOT UNLIKE THE EXPERIENCE OF
MEETING A POLITICIAN FOR THE
FIRST TIME. THE ISSUES OF HOW TO
ADDRESS AND UNDRESS THEM ARE
REMARKABLY SIMILAR.

BODY POLITICS

FIONA PATTEN

'I may be the first former sex worker to be elected to a parliament anywhere in this country. However, I am sure that the clients *of sex workers have been elected in far greater numbers before me.'*
– Fiona Patten, MP, maiden speech, Victorian Legislative Council, 12 February 2015

I suppose it was a coming out of sorts. To my close friends and family, it was not news. Many years before, *The Sydney Morning Herald* had innocently let the cat out of the bag – to those who knew something about the cat and the bag. But this was slightly different. I was publicly admitting to being the fallen woman my granny had always suspected. A Cicciolina of the colonies. An impudent representative of a party that Kerry O'Brien could not even bring himself to name on national television. An outsider with no political pedigree. A clever manipulator of group voting tickets who Antony Green claimed had 'gamed the system', and shamelessly entered the members-only club through the back door. Also I think I was the only woman in Australia who had formed a political party and been elected.

Not only was I falling on my 'sword' in the chamber of Queen Victoria, but I was also making what may have been the first statement about slut-shaming on the floor of a Westminster parliament. And in case anyone thought it wasn't the time or place for such a comment, *Crikey* had just published an article that had backed me to the hilt. In late December 2014 they reported that I had been subjected to some pretty gross slut-shaming as I was being sworn in as a Member of the Legislative Council. Apparently an established and very conservative member of the Council and his staffer (who was only metres above me in the public gallery) were exchanging text messages about my choice for an affirmation rather than an oath on a Bible. 'I thought she'd be swearing on a vibrator,' the MP texted. 'Yeah, I'll bet when she stands up it will look like she sat on an ice-cream,' the staffer replied. And on it went. Unfortunately for both of them, a very well-known political lobbyist happened to be sitting directly above the staffer on the two-tiered leather benches. Being someone with whom I'd had dealings in the past, he discreetly took a photo on his phone of the offending messages and sent it on to the media.

I was more grossed out by the schoolboy mentality that was on display than by the sexual nature of the remarks. The idea of swearing in on a vibrator actually appealed to something dark and pulsating inside me. My sex-industry friends would have been thrilled. I should have passed the MP's name on to Mistress Kate: a prospective client like that with a wild imagination and a love of red leather would be highly valued in the world of gimps and subs. I also thought about placing some of his exact words into an adjournment debate speech or a supplementary question during Question Time – just to make him squirm a little more.

It would not have been the first time that the Parliament of Victoria and the sex industry had been linked. In the 1800s the now infamous Madame Brussels, so named for her nipples (said to be the size of brussels sprouts), ran a brothel only a stone's throw from the Victorian parliament. Apocryphal stories abound of underground tunnels that existed between her establishment at the top of Lonsdale Street and Parliament House. And urban myths regarding the disappearance of the Parliamentary Mace in 1891 suggest that it ended up in one of her chamber rooms, where it was used for some very un-parliamentary business.

My partner, who is prone to believing in unsubstantiated New Age theories from time to time, has even advanced the hypothesis that I may have been Madame Brussels in an earlier life, and that I have now returned to seek vengeance on the God-botherers and nanny-state politicians who closed down my bawdy house in 1907. I'll pass on the theory, though it would make a fabulous movie!

In the end, I would like to think that my short statement in parliament about hypocrisy and cant made the point without labouring it. I liked that some of the men in the chamber appeared to look at their shoes for quite a long time afterwards, while many of the women seemed to smile or laugh in recognition.

However, after the cheering and goodwill of being elected had died down and I was finally being put in my place, I felt somewhat chastened, knowing that I had become that wanker-politician my father had always warned me about. He regularly scorned them in the letters section of *The Canberra Times*. As with having children, I was under no illusion that being elected to parliament was a guarantee of happiness or fulfilment in life. But I did appreciate having a platform to speak out on a number of issues, and the sex-positive lifestyle was high on my list of priorities.

My attraction to the sex and politics game began in earnest when I opened my first business. It was 1988, in the middle of the 'recession that we had to have', and I had just started my own fashion label, Body Politics – which, if you believe in that sort of stuff (like my boyfriend does), could well have been a meaningful portent of my career twenty years later. I rented a small shop in Canberra's iconic CBD hangout, Garema Place, and started selling my own range of clothing. I also invited other independent fashion designers to exhibit with me, which resulted in half-a-dozen young and innovative labels on the racks. Signing a lease to sell independent designer labels during a recession was never going to make me rich, and eventually the business went belly up. Notwithstanding the pain of having to part with my hard-earned money, I actually had a really good time and learnt a lot about business.

Sex workers were about the only people who could afford to buy custom-made indie clothing at that time, and the numbers of them coming through my doors increased. Talking to them about their work and the issues they faced was fascinating, and I became more and more interested in the politics of negotiating sex for money. I had never realised that there was so much involved.

In the early 1990s I became involved with the AIDS Action Council of the ACT and helped out (or, rather, hung out) on their needle exchange bus. I was also helping with and holding events such as early-morning fashion shows for the sex-worker health and advocacy group Workers in Sex Employment (WISE). All night dance-a-thons to raise money for the Wilderness Society were also part of my life then.

I started meeting and having friends who were HIV-positive and who were not getting better. AZT, an early anti-retroviral drug, had just become available but there wasn't much around to be optimistic about. It was the era of the Grim Reaper and a positive diagnosis very often led to significant illness, as well as to discrimination and stigma. Being tested for HIV was not promoted like it is today: the quiet mantra that many of us used to live by was to 'assume everyone is HIV-positive', including yourself.

When Body Politics folded, I managed to get a job as the outreach worker for WISE. It was at a time when Australia was leading the way in responding to HIV/AIDS. Peer education models such as needle exchange programs, AIDS councils and sex-worker organisations (such as WISE) were all well funded by government.

Despite all the gloom of the AIDS virus, it was a wonderfully creative time.

The main part of my job with WISE was to visit all the brothels in Canberra once or twice a week and make sure they were well equipped with safe-sex information, condoms, dental dams, lube, sea sponges and other supplies. Canberra had fourteen legal brothels at that time and most of them had a common room for the workers to relax in and to talk about their work. Twice a week I would spend the evening with them in these rooms, talking about their clients, their working conditions, their mental health, their lives and of course the political framework that defined the way they worked. It was at this time that I had my first 'official' commercial sexual encounter.

At this stage Canberra's brothels were under no legislative imperative to be in industrial suburbs, but many of them found it better to trade among the whitegoods and wallpaper than from a suburban office space or shopping centre. One evening, I was at a well-known brothel in the industrial suburb of Fyshwick, with my bag of condoms, brochures and lube. The red and white neon sign burned bright out the front as I made my way up the rear fire escape – the tradeswoman's entry. Very soon I was talking and smoking around the red laminex table in the common room with a few of the girls. After a couple of minutes one of them got up to do a job, followed soon after by another. Minutes later the doorbell rang again and the last girl I was talking to walked into the reception area, where she chatted to the client and then walked off with him. I was on my own when I heard the receptionist answer the door again: the new client was told that he would have to wait a little while to see someone. I was bored and curious, so I walked out into the reception area, where a reasonably attractive thirty-something man was sitting, a tad nervous and a little expectant. He looked at me as if I was there to greet him but then he sensed that maybe I wasn't part of the establishment. It had been a week since I'd had sex and I remember feeling a little horny. I was also feeling a little broke. I don't know what made me do it but I just jumped in. 'What's your name?' I asked.

'Peter.'

'What do you do, Peter?'

'I'm a plumber.'

'Okay then.' And with that, I ushered Peter the plumber down the hallway and into the 'spa' room. I was slightly nervous but the thought of anonymous sex late in the evening, and extra cash in my pocket, carried me along like a pro.

I took Peter's money, turned the spa on and walked back out to the receptionist with the money. She wasn't quite sure of the protocol with a new worker who was starting unannounced but she took the money gladly. The sex was easy and enjoyable and I ended up doing a few shifts there in the weeks following.

Most sex workers will tell you that the job is actually very easy. It's telling people what you do that's hard. I met quite a few interesting men through the experience – all of them basically grateful that I was prepared to have sex with them and not ask for their phone number after.

I worked on and off over the next couple of years in various brothels and escort agencies, and the sky didn't fall in – although if my granny had found out, it may have! It enabled me to go for working holidays to Cairns, where I could indulge my love of scuba diving on the Great Barrier Reef. I never felt threatened or degraded while doing sex work, and when I compared it with the years of waitressing that I did while studying, I would have to say that sex work was more rewarding in every way. I know that this is not the experience of some workers, especially those who choose to work on the streets, but it was my experience.

In retrospect, sex work was not unlike the experience of meeting a politician for the first time. The issues of how to address and undress them are remarkably similar. The size of their influence, the cut of their jib and their attitudes to women are all there and easy to see. I'd have to say that I probably came up against more discrimination and negative attitudes from politicians than from brothel clients – although occasionally they were one and the same. Brothel clients are often surprisingly courteous, happy to be led and genuinely interested in the lives and welfare of the woman they are interacting with. They seem to suspend their own personal agendas quite a lot while the exchange is taking place, and I'd say that they take a lot of the encounter away with them. This is not the case with male politicians. While they interact with you, their agendas are always there, thrust up hard against you while you try to plead your case. Occasionally, the politicians give way. Okay, my tongue is in my cheek but it's not far wrong!

By the early '90s, sex-work law reform was starting to become a reality in the ACT. There was strong bipartisan support for the decriminalisation of sex work and the ACT government was full of relatively new politicians following self-government in 1989. It was a brilliant environment for me to get my first taste of political lobbying.

Six months after the ACT Legislative Assembly was formed, the independent ACT MLA Michael Moore formed a parliamentary committee that reported on HIV, illegal drugs and prostitution. This led him to table reformist legislation around sex work alongside the shadow health minister, Kate Carnell (now the Australian Small Business and Family Enterprise Ombudsman). The national sex-worker lobby group, Scarlet Alliance, was up and running and had a voice at the table. WISE was an integral member of Scarlet Alliance and, in an effort to demystify the practices of Canberra's brothels, we decided to conduct an Open Brothel Day at which we would open the front doors to any adult who wanted to educate themselves about it all. The day was a huge success. Kate Carnell opened the event at one of the newer brothels in the suburb of Mitchell. Some brothels held sausage sizzles, and most of the 300 people who took advantage of this opportunity to come behind the closed doors were women.

In 1992 I became the first president of the Eros Foundation (now Association) and moved into a wider advocacy role. One of my first duties was speaking at a lunch for women with businesses in Fyshwick. I spoke about the adult industry, the brothels, the adult shops and the large video-duplication warehouses. After the talk they asked if I would take them on a tour. Not surprisingly, none of them had been to a brothel, let alone a porn-manufacturing business. And lo ... the Love Bus was born!

It became a twice-weekly event and over its lifetime we escorted thousands of women through brothels and adult shops. I taught them the difference between a vibrator and a dildo and no-one left the bus without first learning how to put a condom on with their mouth. It was great fun and certainly kept me up to date with the latest porn and vibrator technology. My partner was very pleased to help me with my research. The Love Bus was an example of how a social event can be used to increase sexual pleasure in the community. As always, the most important organ

involved was the brain, and information rather than stimulation the necessary special ingredient.

Having spent twenty-five years in politics, first as a lobbyist
and now as a politician, I am firmly of the view that those
who argue against the sexual life actually don't have one.
Or if they do, it is complicated in ways that ordinary
people just don't understand. The travesty of this is not so
much that these people are missing out but that they seek
to affect others' sex lives by lobbying against pornography
and sex work. Let me explain.

As with many other libertarian issues – such as
marriage equality, drug law reform and physician-assisted
dying – the legalisation of pornography has consistently
drawn majority support in public opinion polls. Yet there
has been no significant law reform in this area, which is
not what one would expect from representative governments. Rather, it suggests that Australia's democracy is
undermined by a highly organised, well-connected and
well-heeled religious minority.

This is best demonstrated by the fact that Australia's
pornography laws are so outdated that material that is
perfectly legal to purchase online, or download, is still
the subject of a major crime offline: adult-shop owners
risk jail time for selling federally classified material. This
situation could not exist if the major parties were adopting
practical and popular policies on adult media. Both Liberal
and Labor have refused to adopt the recommendations of

the Australian Law Reform Commission's inquiry into classification, which were in favour of legalising X18+ films.

Other factors are involved. The feminist arguments against pornography, put forward by MacKinnon and Dworkin in the late 1970s, have been slowly assimilated by the religious right in Australia. This was clearly shown by the arch-conservative independent senator Brian Harradine, who held the balance of power in the Senate over three decades. He was a lobbyist for the Catholic bishops in their efforts to stop abortion, pornography, gay rights, drug law reform and stem-cell research. In his arguments against pornography, he never once invoked religion, instead using the rhetoric of modern feminism and always claiming to be protecting women and children from bad men.

Following Harradine's retirement from politics in 2004, a young 'feminist' adviser he had employed for nearly twelve years, Melinda Tankard Reist, assumed his mantle but from outside the parliament. Tankard Reist is a committed Christian who founded the organisation Collective Shout, ostensibly a feminist group rallying against porn, prostitution, drugs and all the usual vices, and abortion. She works closely with a growing group of sex-negative feminists, and they have successfully lobbied conservative politicians in Australia to the view that young children are being sexualised en masse by the adult industry. They claim that naked depictions of adult women with small breasts or wearing school uniforms are akin to child pornography, and have been responsible for the banning of numerous magazines. Their campaigning has also led to three federal parliamentary inquiries into billboards, customs and classification.

In November 2010, the very conservative and religious Tasmanian senator Guy Barnett was lobbied by the group Kids Free 2B Kids. He was shown a number of magazines featuring legal images they found offensive and asked to do something to stop these magazines coming into Australia. Instead of approaching the Australian Classification Board with a formal submission on whether the levels of restriction on adult magazines were set correctly or matched public opinion, Barnett chose the Senate Estimates forum to grill classification and customs officials about the issue. Exploiting the stigma around sex, he shamed these public servants, as if they were paedophiles for allowing this legal material to come into the country. What followed was two years of mayhem for the importers of adult material, where almost every second shipment of material was red-lined on the docks. We are now at a point where the largest importer of adult films in the country cannot bring in a single copy of an adult film that would be legal in the UK and the USA, even for the purpose of modifying it to meet Australia's already strict code for X-rated material.

This connection of young feminists and old-guard reactionary religious politicians is gathering pace and is a major concern for both feminism and freedom of expression in Australia.

One area in which Australia has been progressive is sex-work law reform. The reforms date back to the 1980s, when street work was legalised in Sydney. Later that decade, Victoria legalised brothels. From there, sex work was decriminalised in most states of Australia. In the beginning this was a feminist-led initiative, but even conservative politicians at the time could see the futility of fining street workers who then had to do more sex work to pay the fines.

In the 1990s more far-reaching law reform was enacted in response to police corruption and HIV. Most of this work took a practical approach to brothels and even street-based sex work. Sadly, this liberalisation is now being challenged by so-called progressive feminists, as well as the churches. Not all the reforms were ideal but in many people's view they were a step in the right direction. One of the most important reforms that Eros was involved in was pushing an amendment to the *Discrimination Act 1991* through the ACT parliament, making it illegal to discriminate against people or organisations on the basis of their occupation. This law has been used by sex workers and people working in the adult-products industry to challenge various injustices: overpriced advertising rates; denial of service from media networks, banks and insurance companies; and even an unfair termination of belly-dancing courses at the local TAFE college.

The issue of sex slavery and trafficking has gained traction in the media and in Australian parliaments. All the liaisons that we have had with sex-worker groups like Scarlet Alliance tells us that real sex trafficking is almost non-existent in Australia, and that allegations of wide-spread trafficking are frequently made up by 'saviour' groups set up to receive lucrative government grants around the world, to help 'trafficked' women. I have long argued that if governments want to reduce the opportunity for exploitation then they need to allow overseas sex workers access to proper working visas, which would enable them to work legally in our brothels, pay tax, earn superannuation and work at licensed brothels. Under an open system like this, crime gangs who want to traffic women would find it difficult to get a toehold in the system, as they would have to offer something that was unavailable from the government.

Amnesty International's latest report on sex work has severely dented the credibility of those who want to adopt the so-called Nordic model of regulating sex work. The Norwegian and Swedish laws are just another form of prohibition – prosecuting clients of sex workers and sending them to jail – and have led to an increase in abuse of and assaults on sex workers. These laws drove otherwise law-abiding men away from the industry, allowing in those who were unafraid of criminality. It was a recipe for disaster that every sex worker in Australia could have told the world, if only they had been given a voice in the issue – rather than the religious or sex-negative feminists.

When I look back on the things that I've stood for in public life, I realise that I could have made easier choices. The public debate on sex remains so heavily influenced by nineteenth-century ideas of love and morality that a large portion of the population is uncomfortable with sex being anything other than a way to reproduce.

The name of the political party I founded still causes quiet outrage in polite society. In 2009, the Australian Electoral Commission had to publish a hefty legal opinion on whether the word 'sex' in a political party's name could be held to be obscene. Our website has been blocked by a number of public institutions, from the Department of Communications to Virgin's airport lounge. People frequently tell me, 'I love your policies but couldn't vote for sex,' and in the lead-up to the last election, two of my candidates were asked to pack up their kit while on the main street of a regional Victorian town – just for displaying a Sex Party A-frame poster. And on it goes.

It's more than moral panic. It's actually a form of insanity. Why is there never the same outrage about using words like 'guns' or 'murder' in the public space? I want sex to be recognised as a healthy, positive part of life. For that to happen, body politics almost needs to be elevated into a ministry all of its own.

IT WAS REAL-LIFE RECON INTO
THE HEART OF ONE OF OUR CULTURE'S
GREATEST PARADOXES – BE SEXY
AND AVAILABLE BUT ALSO
BE FEMININE AND LADYLIKE.

THE CRAZY LADIES

ADRiENNE TRuSCoTT

This is a tale, I think, about colliding, contradictory, heady, dirty, questionable, dangerous, predictable, revelatory, complex versions of a young lady's sexuality finding an ecstatic home in her ever-changing body of desires, doubts and discoveries. Basically.

It's also a tale about a young feminist moving to Austin, Texas, with her very best girlfriend, to study and deconstruct performance with a remarkable and iconic woman, and unexpectedly becoming a stripper to pay for that experience.

It's also a tale about a young waitress having a delicious affair with her co-worker, the bass-playing cook at the local breakfast eatery.

That all of these tales are the stories of the same young woman in the same timeframe is relevant. This doesn't start out sounding like it's about sex, but it is.

When I was about twenty-six, two years out of college and two years into my life of poverty as a performer in New York City, I left the city that never sleeps or pays a living wage to non-visual artists, with my best friend, Rebecca. We headed to Austin, Texas, for a four-month-long workshop in radical performance practice. We were deadset serious about what we were doing as feminists and artists, but also reckless and idiotic and thrilled with one another as friends, comrades, troublemakers – we were accomplices, and my nickname for her was, and still is, Rebellia. We were exactly as broke as two such women would be. We had scrounged up enough money to put down the minimum deposit for the workshop, the first month on an apartment, and enough gas money to drive her old and regularly defunct station wagon nearly 2,000 miles – to a new window onto our respective destinies.

The workshop was a four-month daily intensive of practising the brilliant performance meditations of Deborah Hay.[1] In layperson's terms, this played out as spending four hours every day investigating movement, interaction and 'performance' with prompts like 'My three-dimensional body is made up of 53 trillion cells and every one of them is getting what it needs at every second' or 'I invite being seen getting what I need/What I see is what I need'. Deborah Hay's practices for movement and consciousness are incredibly in-depth and rigorous means of investigating and unpacking your body and mind as you have known them up until then. This was sometimes terrifying and mortifying to do while being witnessed by other people, but they were also doing the same thing – inviting being seen doing it – which was also what made it so liberating.

It may sound academic and esoteric and New Age-y and it was all those things at times, but it was and is a brilliant and life-changing practice. These teachings were accompanied by seemingly more mundane edicts: 'It doesn't matter what you do, it's how you do it' (i.e. perform the most banal cliché – but be rigorous in 'how' you do it); 'Do it like a dog' (by which she meant, do whatever you do, anything, but do it with the same guileless commitment and abandon with which a dog plays fetch. If you just picture that dog, I don't need to explain any more). It may or may not seem odd that these four-hour sessions were frequently hilarious, but humour and a lack of self-censorship (without a lack of self-awareness) are hallmarks of Deborah's work, as well as that of her protégés.

As an extracurricular exercise Rebellia and I had agreed to practise a rule while out socialising, working, etc.: that whenever one of us gave the signal, we had to give a one-minute Deborah Hay–inspired performance at that exact moment, wherever we were – no hedging, no stalling, no faking it. It was mostly to make one another laugh, especially when we were bored or found our environs or the company we were keeping impossibly inadequate (in the judgemental and demanding way twenty-somethings in full thrall to their own possibilities can be). But it made us feel brave and ridiculous and unstoppable.

It also made us feel like it would be funny and not that big a deal to try out a shift at the strip club positioned off the highway behind our charming little apartment.

It wasn't quite as seamless a transition as that sounds. We had jokingly floated the idea as 'probably the only way we can make enough money to pay for the fucking workshop', which was expensive by twenty-something standards – our jobs (I was waitressing; she was baking bread) weren't cutting it. Then Rebellia actually enquired – she found out you just had to show up in an outfit, and your first stint on stage was your audition, or job interview, if you will.

Rebellia, to this day one of the rowdiest, bravest and most fun chicks I know, went first. I was too scared. She returned home laughing, drunk and literally with fistfuls of cash. She said it was so easy it was ridiculous. 'You just get up and dance to Prince!' We got stoned and drunk together that night and practised for each other into the wee hours, laughing uncontrollably at the ludicrous things we would do to appear 'sexy' to the types of men we imagined would be at a strip club called The Crazy Lady in a laid-back town in the middle of Texas.

The next day, after our morning workshop, we went to The Crazy Lady together. Rebellia was already in like Flynn but I still had to audition and I was fucking terri-fied. I had never behaved this way, never tried to be so overtly 'sexy', rarely felt 'sexy' and definitely had never equated this kind of behaviour with 'sexy'. I'm not saying that The Crazy Lady was ground zero for discovering your 'sexy', but it was the first time I had turned the tables on this thing – this ridiculous cultural mandate of female sexuality and whether or not one measured up to it. As a young student in Women's and Cultural Studies and as a 'post-modern dancer', I had really only deconstructed it. And suddenly here I was, a feminist, a burgeoning performance artist taking the stage to perform the most trite version of female sexuality in the very specific service of men's entertainment.

As I mentioned, I was beyond nervous and strangely mortified. The terror stemmed not only from making the attempt, but also from the potential embarrassment of the attempt: that I might try on this culturally received behaviour and then fail at it! Still, with the lifelong guiding principle of 'fake it till you make it', I prepared for my debut. I listened to the DJ announcing my chosen stripper name (Trixie), heard Prince come on, and walked through the curtains to the centre stage, the one with the pole. One song to dance, one song to strip, and then a move to the smaller stage to dance one more song.

Luckily, I had a basis for how to pull this off: I was inviting being seen performing an absolutely banal cliché with the guileless commitment and abandon of a dog playing fetch.

It was fascinating. It was sometimes disgusting. It was revelatory. It was hilarious. In some ways, we did remain 'our true selves' during this experiment. We refused to shave our legs, so we wore back-seamed thigh-high stockings (for the first time EVER), heeled booties, vintage dresses and fur-lined cardigans. It's important to remind you that this was Texas, so every other stripper was wearing a neon G-string and matching pumps, covered briefly by the kind of 'classy', glamorous full-length dresses sold in adult shops. They looked like strippers; we looked like a cross between '90s riot grrrls, your gran and the Artful Dodger. We both started out stripping to either Prince or Barry White – it felt important to us that we were dancing to tunes we loved. However, in a short time I had the good sense to go deeper into the cliché and switch to terrible, but epic, second-wave Aerosmith. Horrible to listen to, great to strip to – like a dog, obvs.

I would never argue that a strip club is a safe space, but there was something safe and liberating about it at that time in my life. I say this knowing I speak from a very particular place: I had a critical lens through which to contextualise what I was doing, and I was very aware that I had made a choice and was doing this as a short-term experiment – I wasn't doing this because I had nowhere else to turn or no other options. Rather, it was real-life recon into the heart of one of our culture's greatest paradoxes – be sexy and available but also be feminine and ladylike. This was not something a 'good girl' does, and it didn't seem like something a feminist would do. But there was something about going to this place every day (another daily practice!), with my best friend as back-up and laugh track, and having a couple of cocktails to disinhibit myself just enough to play out all these loaded and often disempowering versions of 'being sexy'. To be in charge of the mechanism instead of just at the mercy of it; to see how men reacted, to know that I was producing their reactions; to be able to finally measure the distance between my actual self and this kind of embodiment; to know that I had the power to own or disown this weighty garment we're expected to wear. Also, feminist to our core, it was a regular occurrence for us to sit down with the patrons and subject them to a brief lecture on the fundamental problems of exchanging currency for women's bodies. Or, especially if they weren't supplying the requisite one-dollar, five-dollar or (rare) ten-dollar bills in the G-strings of ladies parading for their pleasure, we would make it clear that this pleasure came to them as per the unspoken contract of that financial exchange and such 'friendliness' would not be forthcoming outside of this context. After those interactions the next dance on stage felt like a celebration, a possible fuck-you.

Yes, we were great strippers!

So, every day, we would rise early and go to the studio and practise being present and seen in our 53 trillion cells, trying to strip our performance habits of all artifice, complacency and received cultural behaviours for four hours, and then we would race across town, down some vodka-and-tonics and do the opposite, by actually stripping, for six hours.

And I don't know what it would have been like, or if I'd have ever done it (or had to do it), without the context of my best friend and the workshop. I had these tools, this licence, to both indulge and exploit the experience. I don't know if I would have even allowed myself to act this way without the safety net of the workshop and female companionship, but it was a certain type of introduction to my body, my sexuality and ways of deploying, owning or disowning this sexuality. Also, it would be dishonest not to say that sometimes I felt drunk and sexy and fun and sometimes I also felt gross.

But all this high-falutin' learning and dissecting is nothing if not put into practice, so enter The Chef, the incredibly warm and lovely restaurant cook and bass-player in a local post-punk band. We flirted at work, eventually went out after work, and eventually fell in and out of bed whenever we could. Because of our bonkers schedules, I was often asleep on my shabby futon on the floor when he would use the key I left under the mat to come into my room at some ungodly hour. He'd gently wake me up, and we'd go to town. We just fucked all the time and it was the best sex I'd had in my life up until that point. I just wanted to keep doing it to see what new thing would happen or what new thing I could try or what new feeling I would have. It was boozy, and dirty, sometimes as quick as time and location would allow, and sometimes long enough to call in sick to work and keep going.

And I remember knowing, while being a bit disturbed by the fact of it, that this great sex had to do with the collision and explosion of these three experiences – dancing 'nakedly' (by which I mean 'without artifice') all morning and being asked to push past my limits and fears (creatively, interactively) was cracking me open; and then, with the boldness of the morning's practice in my cells and mind and heart, Crazy Ladying for the rest of the day or night, and all the weirdo proliferation and confusion of sexual energy that produced; and finally, thank god, getting to release it all by shagging this fabulous, incredibly physically generous guy at night.

To say that female sexuality and feminism are two incredibly complex and multi-faceted things is a ridiculous understatement. And we are often expected to have clear boundaries and stances on both fronts. But both are evolving entities and they inform and confuse one another, and I felt lucky to have this period where I got to explore all of it, and to the soundtrack of my choice.

IT'S THE AGE-OLD QUESTION: ARE YOU HAVING GREAT SEX?

HOW IS YOUR SEX LIFE?

MICHELLE LAW

It's the age-old question: are you having great sex? By which I mean, normal sex. By which I mean, are you normal yourself? You know what I mean! Are you a white, cisgender, able-bodied, middle-class, heterosexual person in their thirties with seemingly liberal yet when-it-really-comes-down-to-it deep-seated conservative values that make speed-reading *Fifty Shades of Grey* on your morning commute the pinnacle of your erotic existence? Do you subscribe to the meaningless social expectations forced upon your private life by mass media corporations headed by faceless billionaires dating women younger than their own daughters? Are you all of those things, some of those things, or none of those things? And what does that say about you? Well, you beautiful dummy! Let's find out!

1. Which of these statements best describes you?

a) I am an able-bodied, cisgender, heterosexual person.

b) I am a queer-identifying woman or man, or genderqueer.

c) I am a heterosexual/homosexual person living with a disability.

d) I am an Amazonian warrior queen heavily armed for sexual battle.

e) I am half human, half fish. (You have the wrong book. Return to the ocean and live out the rest of your life in peace, you majestic monster of the sea.)

2. How often do you have sex?

a) Once a year, if I'm in the mood, using the money I receive for Christmas to hire a professional sex worker.

b) If you count fervent masturbation against desk corners as sex, then two to three times a week, excluding my fervent masturbation against desk chairs.

c) Daily. Mama needs her medicine.

d) Bimonthly orgies via Skype with my three younger boyfriends.

3. What is your favourite sexual position?

a) Sideways, reverse cowgirl, while upside down and inside out.

b) The Sumatran Tiger. (Involves tying a leash to your partner's neck and posing for photographs as hired actors rally outside your home citing a petition against animal cruelty on Change.org.)

c) Missionary, with a missionary.

d) Deep Downward Dog. (Doggy style while doing Bikram yoga.)

4. How did you lose your virginity?

a) On my wedding night with my betrothed, atop scattered rose petals on a four-poster bed.

b) With the DJ at a Blue Light disco, to the Spice Girls song 'Viva Forever'.

c) In a steaming carriage, with an amateur artist, aboard a doomed ship in 1912. (If you are a ghost, you have the wrong book. Return to the afterlife and live out the rest of your ghoulish years in peace.)

d) On the top bunk bed in a flea-ridden backpackers, to a drunk tourist in Southern Cross board shorts and a Bintang singlet.

5. What is your preferred sex toy?

a) Fingers 'n' fists.

b) Cucumbers sold for half price as part of Woolworths's 'The Odd Bunch' campaign.

c) A dildo and a butt plug used simultaneously like plungers.

d) So many harnesses that my flesh resembles a deep-sea catch on a commercial fishing trawler.

6. The most adventurous place you've had sex is:

a) In the backseat of my car. While driving.

b) Under a collapsed bridge, like a bedtime-story troll.

c) On set, surrounded by cameras and bored-looking crew members.

d) In my childhood bedroom, which is my current bedroom, because I am forty years old and live with my mother.

7. Perfect sex is:

a) Spontaneous, with a beautiful stranger in a vandalised public restroom.

b) Reclining naked in a leather armchair while receiving cunnilingus.

c) A tender, intimate encounter in a candlelit room with my significant other that lasts for hours.

d) Hard, fast and dirty. BYO Ural.

8. What do you think about during sex?

a) My partner's banging bod against mine.

b) The aquaponics business venture I discussed with my brother-in-law at the last family BBQ.

c) In, out, in, out – that's pretty much it.

d) How Hillary Clinton might have felt when she was pressured to drop her maiden name for the sake of her husband's political career.

Michelle Law

9. Describe the grooming situation 'down there':

a) Like how I take my scotch: neat, with a twist.

b) Waxed almost bare with a landing strip in the shape of Canada. (Their borders are always open.)

c) Could use a trim, but I'm so busy boning up a storm I've just forgotten about it.

d) A HUGE FUCKING BUSH. Literally so thick and incomprehensibly vast it's impossible not to lose anything down there: people's tongues, car keys, groceries, various bric-a-brac. It's the Bermuda Triangle of my body.

10. Choose a sexual fantasy:

a) Licking cheese fondue off my partner's body and being hand-fed Lacteeze tablets like grapes.

b) Seducing the popular dude/chick at my high school reunion and then never contacting them again.

c) Finding a beautiful alien who's crashed to earth in a secluded forest and being wilfully probed.

d) So I walk into a clockmaker's workshop. The clockmaker is alone and the workshop is silent except for the slow tick-tock of the minute hands on the countless clocks he/she has hanging from the walls. We don't speak the same language because we're in Italy, or Spain, or the Mediterranean or some shit. But we communicate with our bodies. We make love so passionately that clocks crash to the floor. Time stops in its tracks. Months later, I discover that

off

169

I am pregnant (although to be honest, it could be to anyone). I give birth to the child, raise it, and when it's old enough we travel back to the clock-maker's studio together. I watch from a distance as the child knocks on the clockmaker's door and the clockmaker answers. He/she takes the child in his/her arms, understanding immediately. I smile bittersweetly, leave the child, and take a couple of expensive-looking clocks with me. Later, I sell the clocks on *Antiques Roadshow* and become a philan-thropic billionaire.

If you answered mostly 'a' ... your sex life is incredible!

You are damn sexy and you know it. From an early age, you worked your sexuality and you've spent years culti-vating a carnally free, happy and fulfilled life. Your open-mindedness and acceptance of others is irresistible.
Your sexual spirit guide: Michelle Kwan's performance to Tosca *at the 2004 US Figure Skating Championships.*

If you answered mostly 'b' ... your sex life is incredible!

You've got one sexually liberated head on top of your shoulders/penis! You don't care about what other people might deem unacceptable because you're confident in your wants and needs, and respectful of your sexual partner(s) and vice versa.

Your sexual spirit guide: The original Broadway recording of Idina Menzel's 'Defying Gravity'.

If you answered mostly 'c' ... your sex life is incredible!

Forget about bad pornography and its unrealistic depictions of sex and derogatory portrayals of women – you know the true meaning of eroticism, and it's exuding so powerfully from your body people can hardly contain themselves around you. Carry an umbrella with you at all times; there's wet weather ahead.

Your sexual spirit guide: Miranda July's exclusive interview with singer-songwriter Rihanna in The New York Time*s.*

If you answered mostly 'd' ... your sex life is incredible!

Your sex life is so incredible it makes me sick. You know that there's no such thing as an 'incredible' sex life because sex is entirely subjective. We all have individual appetites, lust after different sexual practices, and have varying libidos. I salute you. I stand erect.

Your sexual spirit guide: Muriel Heslop and Rhonda Epinstalk saying goodbye to Porpoise Spit in the final scene of the iconic Australian film Muriel's Wedding.

I MIGHT NOT BE ABLE TO
SOLVE A RUBIK'S CUBE BUT I CAN
DEFINITELY FUCK A WOMAN.

DISCOVERING MYSELF

DEIRDRE FIDGE

It was a first for both of us.

We had never touched another's body who resembled our own. We were used to hard, and protruding, but this was soft and enveloping.

Why isn't this more awkward? I wondered. Why isn't there more fumbling and accidental elbowing, or mistimed kisses with clashing teeth, like with most one-night stands? Why does this feel ... normal?

'I'm *really* straight,' I had always emphasised. Those kisses with other girls at teenage parties were just for show, just for the boys. And the ones that occurred at that lesbian bar? Yes, of course. That was just for show, too. Even though nobody else was watching.

My view of both gender and sexuality was still so binary and rigid that the idea of being with someone with a vulva and breasts was unthinkable.

'I wouldn't know what to do down there!' I'd laugh, holding my hands up in comical disbelief as though a vagina was a Rubik's cube. My laugh would be a little too loud, as I realised I was still afraid to give myself pleasure. I was fear-stricken by my own cunt.

Having grown up in a society where female sexuality is almost exclusively shown through the male gaze, it was difficult for me to know what I wanted. In fact, I never asked myself *what do you want?* It seemed safer to seek the same things as my peers – it would provide acceptance and a sense of belonging if I followed the crowd. And so I did. Every now and then, a hint of my true desires would emerge. But it was easier to tell myself that those *risqué* kisses with other young women were for the pleasure of men, and not my own.

After that night of soft and enveloping touches and surprisingly few fumbles, I began to explore my sexuality. It turned out my body knew what I wanted and what to do when my brain didn't. I might not be able to solve a Rubik's cube but I can definitely fuck a woman.

As opposed to when I 'officially' (according to hetero-normative standards) lost my virginity years before, it was so much more exciting once I'd been with a woman. The world looked different; it seemed as though there were more opportunities in my future. The morning after that first encounter, when I awoke in the arms of a woman, my heart felt full – it seemed as though I had found myself, when I didn't even realise I was looking. I was one step away from grabbing a guitar and belting out Melissa Etheridge covers in a park.

Discovering what I liked sexually made me realise how closed off I had been before, not just intimately but in life. I was never the one to apply for a promotion, or ask for a pay rise at work. I would rarely let myself be vulnerable with friends, lest they see me as weak. (I now know the enormous strength in vulnerability.) I would slump my shoulders, literally taking up as little space as possible, in fear of people really seeing me. The fear of rejection was immense. As I continue into my late twenties I am learning that some of the most powerful things women can do are:

- say no
- ask for their needs to be met
- be assertive.

Imagine a world where women-identifying folk do all of the above. For me, it sounds like a blissful and powerful utopia. For a white conservative man, it probably sounds like The Abode of the Damned.

I found myself feeling comfortable using my voice to ask for what I wanted both in and out of a bedroom (or car, or nightclub toilet … look, we've all been there). 'I like it when you touch me here,' a shaky voice emerged from me. It was a pivotal moment when I wasn't rejected for articulating my needs – rather, it was met with hearty acceptance from my lovers. This shy voice that had previously been tiny and hesitant now sang out – I want this,

I like this, I need this. The confidence that grew with sexual intimacy also grew slowly in my general life – I am here, and I have wants and needs. I deserve this pay rise. I deserve to be served at the bar before that pushy man who got there after me. I deserve to take up space.

That young woman I slept with said it was a fun night for her, too. But that night might have been just a bit of drunken fun, just an 'experiment'. Not long after that night, she and her ex-boyfriend reconnected and moved in together.

For me, it marked the beginning of a brand new identity: proudly queer, unashamedly sex-positive, and optimistic about the future.

There has been – and most likely will be – the occasional fumbling moment during intimacy. Not every encounter will be flowing and organic. But when the embrace comes from a place of self-acceptance and openness, it is so much more exciting.

YOU CAN LEARN ABOUT MATHS OR
SCIENCE ON THE INTERNET, BUT WE
DON'T EXPECT YOUNG PEOPLE TO DO SO —
WHY THEN WOULD WE THINK THEY
SHOULD TEACH THEMSELVES ABOUT
SEX?

LET'S TALK ABOUT SEX

ANNE-FRANCES WATSON

Somehow, after years of a semi-nomadic lifestyle and many low-income jobs, I ended up doing a PhD. Whenever the inevitable question 'So, what do you do?' came up in a social situation, and I explained that I would be spending three years researching adolescent sexuality and sexuality education, the response would often include a raised eyebrow or two and an 'ohhhh' – intoned in either a saucy 'tell me more' kind of way, or a prudish 'I don't need to know anymore about that thank you very much' kind of way.

For the people who did want to know more – and they were usually in the majority, because people jump at a sanctioned chance to talk about sex (and academic research makes it seem far more acceptable) – I would explain that I would be going into schools and asking groups of fourteen- to sixteen-year-olds what they knew about topics related to sex, and which of their four main sources (school, parents, friends and the media) they thought they had learnt that from. This would be often met by a proclamation along these lines: 'Well, *I* know the answer to that! Kids know so much more these days! They learn about everything from the internet and the media!'

While you are supposed to go into a research project such as a PhD with a research question that your research will (hopefully) answer, you aren't *really* supposed to assume that you already know that answer. But I have to be honest and say that I, like those people, did think that, because of the internet and the media, the young people I would speak to would be leaps and bounds ahead of where I was at that age in regard to knowing about sex and sexuality.

To some extent I was correct, but mostly I was surprised, and a little bit sad, and very disappointed. I had thought that things would be so different from my experiences growing up and trying to figure out how and why you would have sex. I presumed that, surely, with all of the information so readily available, young people today would know *everything*. What I found was that these teenagers, who were born at least twenty years after me, did know a bit more than I did – but as far as applying that information to their own lives, they were in exactly the same uncharted waters that I had once been in. What's more, those waters are still populated with the sexism and gendered stereotypes that I encountered in my youth.

My parents never had 'the talk' with me. I think, like most parents, they assumed (hoped) that I'd be learning about that stuff at school. Since I was their only daughter, it would have been my mother's responsibility: traditional gender roles largely dictate that fathers give 'the talk' to sons, and mothers give 'the talk' to daughters. Given that my mother married my father when she was nineteen (with my older brother an unofficial 'guest' at their wedding), she had very little previous experience to pass along. Well, I do have three brothers, so she obviously had *some* idea, but she was also fairly religious, and sex wasn't a topic she was comfortable discussing.

This isn't something I hold against my parents. Research has shown that parents often find it difficult to talk to their children about sex and sexuality due to a number of commonly held fears: that they won't know the right thing to say, that talking about it will encourage doing it, or that it's too soon and their child isn't ready to hear it. Parents have these fears for a number of reasons, the primary one being that, unless they grew up on a farm or in a rural area and saw animals going at it, they often didn't get any kind of sex education themselves. (Young people growing up in rural areas have cited seeing animals having sex as the way they learnt about the act.)

Many parents would like to be a source of information for their children when it comes to sex and sexuality. But when parents themselves haven't been taught about something as important as sex, and they have these (quite legitimate) fears about what they should be saying and when they should be saying it, talking to their child about it can seem daunting. This is even more so when it's combined with the stigma around discussing sex – a really fun carryover from the days when religion ruled supreme and sex was considered to be bad unless it was for baby-making. With all of that fear and embarrassment, it is easier for parents to just assume (hope) that schools and the internet will be in a much better position to teach their children about sex.

This avoidance and lack of discussion was echoed in my research. Talking to teens about sex is clearly perceived as a contentious idea, and very few schools allowed me to do this – even with the university's ethical clearance, and the students' and their parents' permission. With the teens I did speak to, it was extremely rare for any of them to say that their parents openly discussed sex with them. Most parents are uncomfortable at the thought of their child having sex (probably as uncomfortable as their child is with the thought of *them* having sex), so even the most positive or progressive of parents can end up promoting abstinence to their child – even when they see that as unrealistic – or sending extremely mixed messages. One young woman I spoke to summed it up this way: 'My parents just say, "Don't have sex, full stop. But if you are going to have sex use a condom. But just don't let it get to us."'

Aside from partnered sex, and very likely for many of the same reasons listed above, the parents of my young participants would either make throwaway comments or avoid discussing anything related to sex and sexuality. This included topics like masturbation, where one parent (a nurse) had an 'awkward conversation' with her daughter that consisted only of the advice to 'use clean hands' if she was going to masturbate.

Parents also rarely discussed consent or healthy relationships – two topics that are interrelated but are rarely treated as such. Consent is often only discussed with young women, and that advice, as my focus groups reported, usually consisted only of girls being told that they can 'just say no'. There are *so* many problems with this, the foremost being that this places young women in a gatekeeper role and divorces any responsibility from young men. It teaches young men that consent isn't their concern. And as the young women told me, if there is any extended discussion of consent, it's usually about strangers at parties, or strangers on the street – but we know that most sexual assault is *not* carried out by strangers. So a little 'stranger danger' training doesn't deal with the fact that saying no can be very complicated, particularly when the person you might be saying no to is someone you like or think you love. This is where young women *and* young men are being done a huge disservice: they're not being taught how to communicate within a healthy relationship.

Parents might be hoping that some or all of these topics will be addressed in schools, but schools can't – or won't – discuss them either. With many schools having a 'one-metre rule' or a 'daylight rule' in effect – meaning that there needs to be either one metre or daylight visible between young people at all times – relationships simply aren't allowed, and therefore don't need to be discussed. And schools won't talk about masturbation – as they can't acknowledge that any kind of sex can be pleasurable. This continued lack of discussion about masturbation in schools (and from parents) confounds me, as it sends the message to young people that it is shameful or wrong – another fun throwback to our uber-religious days – when it is in fact the safest form of sexual activity, as long as you have clean hands ...

I only have two memories of officially learning about sex or sexuality at school. In our Grade 9 science class, we were taught about the wonders of the human body – which did not seem wondrous, and instead seemed pretty gross and completely disconnected from reality. Those pictures of bodies with the skin missing and musculature and flesh in hues of red and blue with yellow fatty tissue were fascinating but weird. If the anatomical pictures weren't of the horrifying skinless variety, they would be cross-sections of bodies so that you could see penises without getting too much of an idea of what they *actually* looked like, other than knowing they dangled down like tiny elephant trunks – which had been cut in half. Still, at least the male cross-section provided some idea – you knew there was a dangly bit that had an upside-down bell-shaped bit on the end, and smaller oval-shaped dangly bits living behind the main dangly bit. The female cross-section gave no such clues about what a vulva would look like. In fact, there was no place to find what a vulva looked like – either a full or neatly trimmed bush were still the main styles of pubic hair at the time, so if you did see a naked lady anywhere, you still had no way of knowing what her bits looked like.

The other occasion where I learnt about sex at school was the actual sex-education class in Grade 10 or 11. This was a one-off session, which was taken by the Film & TV teacher, because – by his own admission – none of the other teachers wanted to do it. My main memory of that class was him telling us the pick-up line he used to attract his wife – something along the lines of 'Nice dress. That'd look great on my bedroom floor.' Classy.

The likely reasons none of the other teachers wanted to teach that class – aside from possibly not having such great pick-up lines to share – are the same reasons many teachers struggle with sex education today. Like parents, the majority of teachers didn't receive any sex education themselves, and they often had little to no training about how to effectively, and without embarrassment, talk to young people about sex.

One topic that does come up in today's sex-education classes is sexually transmitted infections (STIs). When I was growing up, we weren't taught anything about them. In particular, HIV should have been a real concern, but at that time it was seen as something that only gay men would become infected with through sex, and was therefore not discussed. Young people now get versions of the same science classes I received, with anatomical pictures of cross-sections of bodies, but they *are* also taught about STIs. However, as some of the young women I spoke to pointed out, the information they receive is 'scientific' or 'mechanical' – they know about protein coatings of HIV and what an STI can do to a body, but they don't always see that as being relevant to their own lives. The participants spoke to the fact that schools often won't – or can't – acknowledge sex as anything other than a scientific occurrence. And often they feel that schools teaching them about STIs is simply a way to scare them into not having sex. In many cases that's exactly what schools are doing – telling young people horror stories and showing them 'gross pictures' of people with infections, or just bluntly telling them 'you can't have sex'.

There are a number of problems with employing any kind of abstinence message. Young people are curious about sex, and they're pretty sure it isn't as bad as they're being told it is, so they will often go ahead and try it out for themselves, or at least try to learn more about it. Many young people will seek out this information from friends or the media – particularly that 'internet' we've all been hearing about, which I'll discuss a bit later. The problem with getting information from friends (who young people count as one of their trusted sources, while also taking everything they say with a grain of salt) is that this advice is usually based either on experience, or on information that the friends themselves have cobbled together from their other sources. Experiential learning is valid in some contexts, but when it comes to sex, learning by doing, without vital information about safe practices, leads to *un*safe practices.

I did have one friend at school who was taking part in some experiential learning, but I was too embarrassed to ask her about it. I don't think my parents had any idea that any of my friends were doing it. Aside from (mistakenly) assuming that I would learn about sex at school, my parents probably saw little need to talk about it with me because I was the girl who always had her nose in a book, or stayed up late to watch *Star Trek: The Next Generation*. When my father would wake and hear the unmistakable sounds of Captain Picard and his crew, he would yell out, 'ANNE-FRANCES, TURN THAT FUCKING TV OFF AND GO TO BED!' and I would turn the volume down until it was barely audible and sit directly in front of the tiny television. Cross-legged, with my face nestled in my hands, I would stare dreamily (and slightly cross-eyed) at some of my great TV loves of that time – bearded Commander Riker (Jonathan Frakes), bald Captain Picard (Patrick Stewart), and baby-faced (and much more age-appropriate) Ensign Wesley Crusher (Wil Wheaton). Thinking back on it now, I can only assume that my love for these characters might be one of the sources of my penchant for bald, bearded, or youthful-looking men (I'm yet to find the man who is the perfect triumvirate, but I live in hope).

Prior to *Star Trek: The Next Generation*, my celebrity crushes had mostly consisted of various TV and movie stars, and musicians. New Kids On The Block was my version of The Beatles, Backstreet Boys, or One Direction. Their posters, gently and lovingly removed (so as to avoid the dreaded tearing of the faces by the poorly situated staples) from *Smash Hits* and *TV Hits*, joined members of the Brat Pack – particularly Charlie Sheen – on my walls. Charlie was the recipient of my first – and only – fan letter in which I declared my deep love and admiration for him and his acting abilities. To Charlie, that love and admiration was only worth an impersonal black-and-white photograph of him, signed with a gold pen – which did make it feel a bit more special – and I still have it in its pristine condition today.

While I did have the beginnings of sexual feelings towards these poster idols, their movies and music and TV shows didn't provide me with much quality information about sex.

In fact, the movies and TV shows that I loved at that time often have extremely questionable narratives upon re-examination. I loved *Sixteen Candles* as a teenager, but when I re-watch it now I'm absolutely horrified – like *Revenge of the Nerds* and so many of my other beloved teen movies, it uses non-consensual sex as a joke or a punch-line. At that time, female characters had little sexual agency: they were often the object of a male character's desire, and sex was hardly ever about what they wanted. Women were prizes or trophies to be won by men, and sex was a conquest. Movies and TV shows with a young female protagonist were very rarely about her wanting to have sex – the most she would want was a perfectly chaste first kiss. (There are, of course, exceptions – like *Dirty Dancing*, which I really should watch again for the hundredth time.) So, unless I watched some more adult movies, I was unlikely to find out anything interesting about sex. Thankfully, there were magazines like *Dolly* and *Girlfriend*.

We didn't have much money when I was growing up – after all, my parents had four children to feed – so my brothers and I didn't get any of the mythical 'pocket money' that I heard so much about from other kids. This meant that I had to squirrel away birthday money from my grandparents, and for a while I was reluctant to spend it on magazines that weren't as rich with posters as *Smash Hits* and *TV Hits*. Luckily the city library subscribed to *Dolly* and *Girlfriend* for me (and all of the other povvo teenage girls), and I could borrow up to six at a time. When I got a bit older I did use my birthday and Christmas money to subscribe to *Dolly*, and for that year it felt amazing to have the magazine arrive each month, knowing that it was all mine and I could rip open the Dolly Doctor sealed section for myself. I once met the Dolly Doctor, Dr Melissa Kang, at a sexual health conference, and I think I might have made that excited high-pitched squeal that only dogs and dolphins can hear.

Dolly was my first source of sex education. It provided me with information about masturbation, and assured me that my furtive fumblings in the shower were perfectly normal. The stigma around masturbation didn't allow me to share or discuss this with anyone, but I felt slightly less shameful about doing it. Sadly, *Dolly* wasn't allowed to tell me how to make my fumblings more effective – they had (and still have) ridiculous rules about not being allowed to give any kind of instruction – so I only learnt about that a couple of years later in *Cleo*. It took a lot of practice before I finally figured out how to get myself off, and it makes me a little sad to think of all of those wasted years where I could have been having orgasms – I might have made a more concerted effort if I'd realised how good it was, but que sera sera. It was also *Dolly* that told me how I could see a vulva – my own, with a mirror.

There's constant debate about the media and its place in sexuality education. Most of the research in this area has explored the potential effects of media consumption or media exposure on young people's sexual development. The models derived from these media-effects studies often claim there is a causal relationship between young people being exposed to sexual content in the media and becoming sexually active – the old 'monkey see, monkey do' scenario. This is clearly an over-simplification – there are many different media-effects models and theories, and they all have their own nuances and approaches – but largely, the cause-and-effect relationship is what they boil down to.

The problem is that these models only ever show a correlation rather than a causal relationship, and often fail to address three key issues in young people's consumption of media – issues that may affect the correlation being observed.

First, they don't allow for the fact that young people have a *choice* in which media they consume, and that they choose media that presents information and viewpoints that seem most relevant to them. In other words, media-effects models often disregard young people's agency – they aren't just passively watching whatever is on, but are choosing what they want to see and hear.

Second, these models rarely take into account *how* young people consume media. With the advent of mobile devices, they may be consuming up to three or four different types of media at once – they could be watching TV, while using social media on their phone, while also watching videos on YouTube. So the amount of attention paid to any one of those sources is probably not going to be quality attention, and would therefore dilute or discount any potential effects – they might completely miss any sexy bits in that TV show because they're too busy commenting on their friend's latest Instagram selfie.

Finally, these approaches don't provide a model for understanding how young people *interpret* the media they consume – which is often in ways quite different from those expected by researchers. In one study, researchers watched television shows that had large teen audiences, and coded how many times there was anything they classed as 'sexual content' (this is another simplification, but you get the gist) – they found quite a lot of it.[1] A different study then used the same television shows, but asked teenagers to do the coding. The teenagers found far fewer instances of sexual content – there were obviously differences between what they thought was sexual and what the researchers thought was sexual (or what the researchers thought that teenagers would think was sexual).[2] Young people's interpretations can further vary according to a number of factors such as their age, race, and cultural and religious background. This calls into question a large number of media-effects studies because they rely on a standardised coding system that is devised by researchers without consultation of the target audience – young people.

Many of these researchers see young people as being in need of protection from seeing anything sexual – in case they get ideas. There are, however, theorists who recognise young people's agency, and point out that instead of young people starting to explore their sexuality because they have consumed sexual media content, the opposite is more likely – that those who are curious about sex, or who have started experimenting sexually, are looking for more information and therefore seeking out media that has sexual content. This ties in with other research that has shown that when young people encounter sexual content or material that is beyond their developmental stage, they don't understand it or engage with it – they might see something sexual and think *that's weird*, ask what is happening or move on to doing something else.[3]

So, essentially, young people (or people of any age really) learn about sex from the media when they are *ready* to learn about it. I didn't start reading *Cleo* or *Cosmopolitan* until I had finished high school because I was a late bloomer sexually – I was interested in sex, but I knew I wasn't ready for it. I didn't feel the need to know too much about it beyond what I read about 'throbbing members' in the Mills & Boon books I stole from my mum's bedroom. As smart as I was, most of the sexual content either went completely over my head, or was of little interest to me.

This self-selection was also true for a number of the participants in my focus groups. Girls of the same age were at different levels of sexual development: some were still reading and enjoying *Dolly* or *Girlfriend*, but others felt those magazines were too young for them and had moved on to *Cleo* or *Cosmopolitan*. These young women also attested to how much of their sexual information they received from these magazines: like me, this was where they received the bulk of their sexual education.

I was disappointed to learn, though, that masturbation was still seen as 'dirty'. Although magazines told these young women that masturbating was normal, they weren't getting that message from many other sources – and the silence around it made it seem shameful. My participants were clearly experiencing some cognitive dissonance because they would often say it was dirty or wrong or weird for girls to do it immediately after saying that they knew it was normal. Some of these young women didn't know *why* you would masturbate – or how to do it. Many of them thought it was 'desperate', because they believed that if you had to masturbate, it meant you couldn't get a boyfriend.

It deepened my sadness to hear that many of these young women believed they needed a partner to provide sexual pleasure. The sadder fact is that, because many of them didn't really know how to do that for themselves, an equally uneducated teenage boy was probably not going to know how to either. This gendered messaging around sexual pleasure was fairly prevalent – for girls, it was seen as something that had to be given to you by a boy, instead of something you could take for yourself.

As I said at the beginning, although many of these young women were ahead of me in knowing about sex – and some of them were *way* ahead of me in that they had already had sex – the information they were receiving was still often sexist and confusing. They were getting some great information from magazines and TV and movies and the internet, but their parents and schools were still counter-acting these messages. The participants in my research had high levels of media literacy – media literacy is an area in which Australian schools are world leaders – but often this literacy told them to be highly critical and distrustful of what they saw in the media, and they often spoke about it as not being 'real'. This is all well and good, except when the media is the only place that's giving you decent and credible information.

To return to the subject of the internet, and how young people should know so much about sex now because of the digital age: this idea bothers me for three reasons. The first is the media literacy I spoke about – many young people question the credibility of any information found online. The second is, just because the information is out there, it doesn't mean they know how to find the *right* information. And the third reason: should young people really have to teach themselves about the nuances of healthy and pleasurable sexual relationships? You can learn about maths or science on the internet, but we don't expect young people to do so – why then would we think they should teach themselves about sex? Learning about healthy and respectful (and pleasurable) sex requires context and guidance, which are largely missing from their sources of information about sex.

This all sounds a little bit depressing.

And it might have been.

Except that this research took place a few years ago now, and in that time, there has been the beginning of an amazing shift in the media. Now there are sex-positive TV shows, web series, feminists and comedians. *Orange Is the New Black* has provided some quality education about sex and sexuality – and anatomy (even I learnt a few things). Ilana and Abbi from *Broad City* aren't afraid to sexually experiment – with themselves and other people – say what they want, and get what they want. Amy Schumer is open about masturbating and sex – enjoying it, wanting it, and wanting it to be good. She talks about birth control and condoms and STIs, and about needing to check whether you have stray toilet paper in your vagina before having sex – and telling your sexual partner that that is what you're doing as you head into the bathroom.

With women like this in the media – women who are *real*, and see sexual pleasure as something that they deserve and are entitled to – I wish that I could go and talk to more young women to see if things have changed for them and how they think about sex and pleasure. I suspect that things *have* changed for the better. But that doesn't mean we should rely on the media to teach young people about sex. We can certainly use the media as a tool in the sexuality education toolkit – but that toolkit should be in the hands of schools and parents.

The single best thing that parents can do is to start talking to their children about sex and sexuality from an early age. This will make it more comfortable and less awkward over time. There are great (and free) resources available like *Talk Soon. Talk Often.* that take you through what you should say and when.[4] Schools need to be given a mandate to have realistic and open discussions with young people, and acknowledge that sex is supposed to be fun and pleasurable. In the Netherlands, where there is an openness about sexuality – and comprehensive sexuality education is provided from a young age – teen pregnancy and STI infection rates are among the lowest in the developed world.

By using popular media as a jumping-off point, schools and parents can have regular and ongoing discussions with young people about sex and sexuality – not one-off box-ticking exercises with dodgy pick-up lines. If we can end this cycle of stigma and silence around sex, we will be happier and healthier for it.

IN TRUTH, LOVE IS NOT A TURN-ON.
REAL, DEEP LOVE IS LIKE GOING
TO CHURCH: SOMBRE, MOVING, AND
SPECTACULARLY TERRIFYING.

SEX AND LOVE, BERLIN 2016

AMY MIDDLETON

She has already proposed – although I've told her I need a 'real' ring to wear, rather than this wound-up wire number.

We can't legally get married, but that's not the point. The point is that we are going to try and stay together for the rest of our lives.

Just her, and me. For life. It's a daunting, beautiful prospect.

We sit in a courtyard, at a restaurant in Berlin. Europe is coming out of peak tourist season, but it's still warm. We are the only people in the *Biergarten*.

It's just after 8.00 pm. We left our hotel room to find a bar we'd heard about called Bassy Cowboy Club – a music venue, because that's where we find our people. When we got to Schönhauser Allee, the bar was shut. Wanting a drink, we walked a block or two and found this *Biergarten*, attached to a Spanish restaurant.

We're sitting outside among white plastic chairs. The ground shines with rain, and the garden is surrounded by towering apartment blocks. Behind us, we can see the locals eating tapas through the windows of the restaurant.

'Let's get cocktails,' she says, beaming at me. 'I want a pina colada!'

She's wearing a black shirt, creased and ill-fitting after a day of walking between monuments in the humid air. Her shirt doesn't quite match her shorts – it's the practical, easy style of someone who has squashed two months of outfits into a suitcase the size of a drawer.

I've managed a dress, but nothing fancy. It's a black basic that suits day and night wear – a traveller's staple.

'Coconut and alcohol, ew,' I say. 'We can't afford cocktails.'

I've taken to agonising over every dollar we spend, calculating the exchange rate into AUD to figure out how many meals we're sacrificing when we get home, poor and coming down from travel.

It's a very romantic attitude.

But my girlfriend is an expert arm-twister. She can make digging in the garden sound like a rollercoaster ride. When the waiter brings our cocktails, I try her pina colada first, and then my Long Island iced tea. The pina colada is better, and she lets me drink most of it.

Travel to Europe promises so much. You have visions of yourself in montage, backed by a soundtrack, as if that's how life plays out. You expect perfect lighting, filters on skies. You imagine frolicking in beautiful clothes around Paris or Rome, in calm ecstasy, where every coffee is sipped in a cobblestone lane, and every meal is eaten on a piazza at sunset.

But when you get there, you are still you. If you aren't carefree at home, you probably aren't carefree when you travel. If your internal monologue bothers you, or you're plagued by anxiety, or you bicker with your partner about work or future plans, all these things – and more – await you overseas.

People don't become more romantic in Venice, or more beautiful in Copenhagen. We are who we are, and we can only work with what we've got.

We're at another venue. It's grungy and dimly lit, with an American punk behind the bar, and a photo of AC/DC on the wall. We feel at home here, sitting on stools next to the beer taps.

We can smoke inside, and I'm thrilled – my girlfriend, not so much. I order a Campari and soda, and a beer for her, and breathe easy when the tab is less than five euros.

A German guy sits next to us at the bar. His name is Sven, he's twenty-eight, and he comes to the bar a lot, he says.

Sven is friendly, and wonderfully German. He has drunk, gentle eyes. He buys us a round of drinks, and my girlfriend quickly reciprocates, ordering two beers for herself and Sven before he's finished his glass. Sven's English isn't amazing, and he employs the Google Translate app on his phone.

How long are you in town? Sven types.

I take his phone. *Three more nights.*

I'd love to show you around.

A distant alarm bell buzzes in my head. I give a polite smile, and change the subject. *Have you always lived in Berlin?*

When my girlfriend speaks to Sven, she is bold. She talks loudly in her broad Australian accent, and doesn't watch to make sure he's keeping up. She tells him jokes, and then laughs at them. He treads more carefully with her.

She buys another round and employs her poor German, for the first time, to ask where the toilet is.

'Sven!' she says. '*Wo ist die Toilette?*'

While she's in the bathroom, Sven asks again if he can show us around Berlin. He suggests a time and place to meet, and I start to feel a heady mix of anxiety and agitation.

We have plans tomorrow, I type. *But thank you! That's very kind.*

He persists. *How about Wednesday? I'll meet you at your hotel.*

I glance towards the bathroom door. *I don't think it's going to work, our schedule is pretty full. But thank you!*

When my girlfriend returns to her seat, Sven says his goodbyes and swans out of the bar.

She waves, 'Bye, Sven!' and turns to me. 'Another Campari?'

There's something tenuous about travelling with one partner. Two people, alone in an unfamiliar country – that makes a tough foundation for a good time.

Silences can feel strained. Travel mishaps can feel heavy, even overwhelming. There is pressure on travellers to *enjoy yourself*, *get amongst it* and *make the most of every day*.

A shitty travel experience can feel like a reflection of self – as though you weren't capable of finding fun, or you were too sensitive to fully let go, or too precious or uptight to get into the spirit of the local culture.

Too frightened to hang with the locals. Too careful to join a stranger on a tour of a foreign city, even when he's offering to meet you at your hotel.

This pressure can feel exaggerated being in a couple. You run the risk of building an echo chamber of shame, resentment and unmet expectations.

Overall, travel is rarely as sexy as it promises to be. Hotels aren't the clandestine boudoirs we are promised by French films. They are utilitarian: a place to rest your blistered, stinking feet, where a hundred or more other people have slept, drooled, spat and sweated before you.

The American punk bartender has learnt our names. I've moved to whiskey sours, and it's past midnight.

My girlfriend spots a notable Aussie musician across the bar. She says his name with reverence, watching for my reaction. I wouldn't recognise him if I tripped over him in *die Toilette*, but I know his name and, like everyone, I know his music.

The musician makes eye contact with me over the bar, so I give him a wave. My girlfriend walks over to say hello. They have mutual friends, plus we're all Aussie, so he invites us to sit with him.

I'm still smoking, but my rolling ability is waning. My girlfriend hates the habit, but when I pass her the pouch, she rolls me a perfectly slim cigarette as she talks music with the semi-celeb beside me.

He directs all his responses to me, and only looks at her when she asks him a question.

'Have you spent much time in Berlin?' she asks. She doesn't care about – or actively doesn't notice – the way he stares at me. 'I love the way no-one cares what you look like here. You can be whoever or whatever the fuck you want, and feel totally comfortable.'

'Believe me, it used to be better.' He looks wistfully at the shelves of liquor behind the bar.

He starts recounting his years on tour in Berlin in the late 1980s. The girls, the bands, the drugs. While he talks, he smiles and shakes his head, to nobody but himself, as though no-one could possibly understand how *crazy* things got back then.

'These days, every second musician is in Berlin,' he

says. 'And I can't walk down the street without running into someone from home.'

He gestures rudely at us. I retaliate with the ammunition of ten shots of liquor. 'How awful,' I say. 'Finding people from Australia, while you're in one of the cultural capitals of the world. Imagine that.'

He manages to laugh at himself, and then says it's time he went home. He gives me a long look, waiting for me to agree. Perhaps it's worked for him in the past, but I've had my hand on my girlfriend's thigh for the past half-hour.

'You'll have one more round!' she orders him. He sits obediently back on his stool.

Travel has a way of highlighting your fears. I'm perpetually frightened of domestic doldrums, the loss of desire – and this fear is never more acute than when we are on the road.

What happens when you've been with someone for five years? Or ten? It's inevitable that lust flickers and dims, like an old lightbulb. That level of attraction and magnetism that existed in the beginning is not sustainable.

I've always thought that when you connect with someone, you join together and create a new space, a little empty pocket of the world just for the two of you. At first that space is filled with lust: the aching need that makes you skip work, miss friends' birthdays, eat poorly and generally make bad life choices. It's the stuff procrastination is made of.

As you get to know each other, that space begins to fill. It gets crowded by nights spent in emergency rooms, tough conversations at family funerals, and hours following your lover through shops you don't give a shit about, just to be near them.

Sex isn't what it used to be. The initial desperate desire is replaced by something else. It's replaced by love.

In truth, love is not a turn-on. Real, deep love is like going to church: sombre, moving, and spectacularly terrifying. With love comes the troubling realisation that you could very easily, very quickly, lose everything you care about, everything you need to survive. It's a thoughtful, frightening experience. It is standing on the top of a cliff where the view would be amazing, if only you could stop thinking about falling.

Eventually, you don't need to desperately explore someone, because you've learnt who they are. You know their smells, how their moods change with stress, how their diet affects their sleep.

You don't need to stay up all night talking, because you've heard all the stories about their past lovers – at least, the ones they're willing to tell you.

You don't need to call them throughout the day, because you know they'll be there when you get home, and what they'll say when they see you, and in what tones.

Once you know someone is going to be there, you stop having to look for them.

Three cognacs later, the muso is finally ready to stagger out of the bar. It's 2.30 am and we are drunk, but not as drunk as him. Nothing makes you tipsier, it seems, than recounting your glory days to an indifferent audience.

'I'm going, I'm going,' he says, swaying for the door.

'So go already,' I tell him. He gives us a drunken wave as he exits, and my girlfriend beams.

'What a wanker,' I say.

The barman looks at me, shocked. 'Do you know who that was?'

My girlfriend nods, wide-eyed, and they share a silent moment between fans.

We stumble in the direction of our hotel. Never the navigator, I blindly follow my girlfriend. I think out loud about the sorts of people we gravitate towards just because they're from the same geographical location as us.

I tell her about Sven, how he offered us a guided tour of Berlin, how I was tempted, but cautious, and that sometimes I wish adventure wasn't such a gamble.

That's when she sees the construction site.

It's a building covered in scaffolding, about ten storeys high. The bricks are dark, and the layers of scaffolding are separated by temporary ladders. We're on a residential street about four blocks from our hotel in Mitte.

'You want to climb up to the top?' she asks, her eyes shining.

'No,' I say.

'Yeah! Let's climb up there, like Donkey Kong!'

Like a child, I'm lured by the promise of fun and, next thing I know, I'm scaling a ladder on a rickety building site, watching my feet with drunken over-caution.

After four floors, I've lost all fear. I'm high on adrenaline and the view of Berlin that's sprawling out next to us.

We climb another couple of ladders, and walk around the scaffolding to the east side of the building, about six storeys up.

We look down at the road, and across Berlin at the lights, the dark buildings and clusters of trees. I start rolling a smoke.

She says, 'We should have sex up here.'

I look at her. I don't say anything. I light my smoke and take a couple of drags, then she puts her hand up my dress.

It's the first time we've ever had sex outside. As I make her come, standing against a wooden wall, I look over her shoulder at the dark sky. With my hands, I thank her for her sense of adventure. I feel grateful for our trust in each other, and for the low cost of alcohol in Europe. I even feel grateful for that dickhead musician, because he united us, made us laugh, and reminded us that we're empowered and in love, which is better, in the end, than any crazy scene or fleeting tour.

I finish my cigarette and we start back down the ladders. My legs are shaky from alcohol and nicotine, and from coming in the dark sky, six storeys above Europe.

Climbing down the last ladder, she awkwardly lets go and tumbles drunkenly out of the scaffolding, landing hard on her knees.

I try not to smile, but she says it doesn't hurt, and we both end up bent double with laughter, our faces going red inches from the cracked footpath.

In the morning, we inspect her wounds in the safety of our white sheets. On her knee is a mottled gash that scars, even after we return home from Europe. It will remain visible there – a reminder of a *Biergarten*, a bar and our building site – for the rest of our lives.

THE INTERNET GAVE ME
THE TOOLS TO BEGIN MY OWN
SEXUAL REVOLUTION.

GETTING IT ONLINE: FEMINISM, INTERNET DATING AND SEX

GISELLE AU-NHIEN NGUYEN

We sat by a river in Chicago, legs dangling off the pier, with a backpack full of cheap beer. He showed me his tattoos and I thought he was made of magic. When it started to rain, we ran back to his house, holding hands as it bucketed down.

Inside the tiny ramshackle sharehouse, he dried me off with a towel, and we sat holding hands watching a documentary, and finally he kissed me, and we went to his bedroom and fucked, and it was nothing and everything all at once.

It was the first time I'd slept with someone I didn't know, two months after my long-term relationship had ended. I was intoxicated by how this boy was first a name and a series of photos on my screen, and then a number on my phone, and then a mouth on every part of me, and then a goodbye kiss in the doorway at 1.30 am before I got an Uber back to my hostel to make my eight o'clock flight to Los Angeles in the morning.

So this was what it felt like, I thought. The freedom to do anything, to be anyone. To shake off the shame that my conservative childhood told me I should feel towards loveless sex; to become the architect of my own pleasure.

That night, the penetrative sex had hurt and we'd had to stop, but he hadn't judged me – he'd just held me.

And that's when I realised that, though love had faded from my life, I could find acceptance in the most unexpected places.

★

I've never fucked someone I didn't meet online – how's that for a millennial statement?

I met my first two boyfriends on the music website Last.fm and Twitter; the relationships lasted one year and half a decade, respectively. They were the second and third boys I'd ever kissed, coming, as I did, from a conservative Vietnamese family where I was taught that any kind of sexual act was reserved for love.

It was during the second relationship that I discovered feminism, at twenty-one, and slowly my worldview began to change. I'd previously judged women who were openly sexual, but suddenly I found myself curious, envious. This was only compounded by my continuing struggle with the sexual pain disorder vaginismus, thanks to my first boyfriend's lack of patience or kindness. Sex was trauma-tising for me, and I didn't want it to be. I wanted to know how it felt to be sexually free – to be in control of my own body.

The internet gave me the tools to begin my own sexual revolution.

*

Internet dating was once heavily stigmatised, seen as a place for freaks and weirdos who couldn't get laid in real life to find other freaks and weirdos who couldn't get laid in real life. My parents talked about people meeting online with the kind of hushed terror usually reserved for discussing murders and kidnappings, despite the fact that my mother's favourite film was *You've Got Mail*.

These days, no-one bats an eyelid when others mention meeting their romantic or sexual partners online. It's a logical shift, seeing that so much socialising, whether platonic or romantic, happens on the internet – from the early, heady days of ICQ and MSN to today's world, where social invitations are often extended only through Facebook events. Sex therapist Cyndi Darnell believes that the ubiquity of online dating has opened up new possi-bilities for women, especially in a metropolitan, western context.

'A lot of people live online these days, and so extending dating into that world has created not only a new way of interacting, but it's also created a new culture – it has given women more power and more choice and more agency,' she says.

'The notion of "swiping" [on Tinder] is not brand new – back in the day when people used to date in more conventional ways, when you'd sit in a bar, you'd still be swiping, technically, but you'd be swiping with your eyes, not with your finger. Now you've got the convenience of doing it in your own home.'

Tinder and similar apps act as an extension to pre-existing social networks like Facebook, requiring users to have accounts with those sites to sign up, then showing them their mutual friends and interests with potential matches. According to sexuality researcher Joni Meenagh, this is a major part of why these services have taken off in such a huge way.

'For women, there is still a lot of stigma attached to having casual sex, particularly with "strangers",' she says. 'Having this pool of people who are kind of known can make them seem like a safer option than hooking up with some random person at a bar, and I think that's why Tinder has been so successful – because it's linked to your Facebook, it contextualises people who would otherwise be "strangers on the internet" within a social network.'

And it's not just strangers you can meet – these apps can also re-ignite long-ago connections. Once, I hooked up with a guy I'd known half a decade earlier when I lived in a different city. We matched on Tinder when he happened to be in town, and I doubt we would ever have even seen each other again, let alone had sex, were it not for that fateful right-swipe.

'The internet allows us to maintain passive connections with people who we aren't close to, like people we knew from school or an old job, or people who we met briefly,' Meenagh explains. 'Social network sites have opened up the possibilities for dating and casual sex.'

The idea of unattached sex is certainly not new, but with the advent and ever-increasing dominance of social media and online dating, it's become a whole new beast. As well as the traditional services, there are those especially for people of certain races and religions (JDate, Christian Connection, Asian Avenue), the LGBTI community (Grindr, PinkSofa, HER, TG Personals), people with STIs (Positive Singles), kinksters (FetLife) and even lovers of beards (Bristlr) – as sex-advice columnist Dan Savage often says, there's a lid for every pot.

Where before, many women were peering out at the world of sexuality through a crack, the window of possibility has now been blown wide open.

★

Growing up in the age of chat rooms and MySpace, I was no stranger to talking to men online. The internet was where I learnt how to be sexual, through heated secret cybersex sessions with internet boyfriends (earning me a ban on Neopets) and lengthy discussions about sex and bodies with friends I only knew through the screen. It had always been a safe place for me to experiment outside the boundaries imposed upon me by my strict upbringing.

I signed up to Tinder and OkCupid in 2014 to get over the breakup of my second relationship, which had lasted five years. I'd previously been a teenager living with my parents and cybering on a dial-up connection without the possibility of meeting up with these people, but now I was twenty-five and living independently, a thousand kilometres from home. The possibility of taking my sexuality from URL to IRL became a whole lot more plausible – I was about to break the wall and let the fantasies cross over into my physical world.

I set up my profiles and wrote down the key points about myself I thought potential matches should know.

Feminist.

Vegan.

Not looking for a relationship.

And then the messages came rolling in.

'You had me up until feminism.'

'Make me a sandwich.'

'Why are you on Tinder if you're a feminist?'

'I've always wanted to fuck an Asian chick.'

'Is cum an animal product?'

★

Jamie was twenty-three – three years my junior. I'd never been with someone more than a year younger than me, but he was funny and cute, and we liked the same music. He'd also recently broken up with someone and was looking for casual sex, just like I was.

We met up at the pub on a Sunday afternoon and chatted about bands over ciders and parmas. The vibe was good and I was attracted to him, so I asked him to come back to mine.

We lay in my bed, fully clothed, continuing to chat for a bit. Neither of us wanted to make the first move. Eventually we kissed, but it was still a while before things really took off. He seemed shy, scared, nervous. It was like both of our first times all over again.

He kissed down my body and I kissed down his. We moved like silk, and then like a storm – soft and slow, hot and heavy. But suddenly, as our fucking became more vigorous, my stomach felt queasy.

'Hey, can you stop?'

He didn't stop.

'Did you hear me? I told you to stop.'

'Yeah, but I was just finishing.'

Holding back tears, I put on my clothes. 'I think you should leave.'

★

It's no secret that being a woman on the internet is exhausting at the best of times. When you add in the element of openly seeking sexual or romantic connections, things get a little darker – I genuinely believe Unsolicited Dick Pic would be the scariest possible

Halloween costume – and when you add unabashedly identifying as a feminist on dating sites to that, you've got the perfect storm.

'I could buy a month's groceries if I had a dollar for every man whose opening line on a dating app was them proudly declaring that they're a feminist, as though it's a golden ticket to get in my pants,' says Ophelia, a twenty-year-old plus-size queer woman. 'On the other hand, I could buy a house if I had a dollar for every threat or insult I've received pertaining to either my feminism or body positivity.'

This dichotomy is perfectly represented through the popular Tumblr page Male Feminists of Tinder, flooded with screenshots of men brandishing feminist buzzwords with all the glee and desperation of puppies waiting for head pats, and the Instagram account @feminist_tinder, collecting examples of all the ways feminists are harassed on Tinder for their proud, open political identification.

Tinder cofounder Whitney Wolfe launched Bumble in 2014 as a feminist alternative to the popular dating app. The premise is simple – women are in the driver's seat and have to send the first message within twenty-four hours of a match, after which time it expires. No more unsolicited dick pics! No more uninvited aggressive sexual messages! And for women seeking women, anyone can start the chat. Sounds like a dream, right?

'I don't know that an app is going to shift something that is an entrenched cultural way of thinking,' Darnell says. 'In terms of actually shifting the way that people interact with each other online, that has to come down to a level of cultural respect, and we still struggle with having respectful connections. When sex becomes involved, people seem to lose their manners – it has a lot to do with the lack of respect that we have for sex in general, which is informed by gender.'

Many of the women I spoke to expressed similar frustrations about online encounters with people – largely cisgender men – who are entitled and rude when it comes to sex. Disappointingly, many of the culprits identify as feminists themselves.

Harriet, twenty-four, shares her poor friends-with-benefits experiences with self-identifying feminists and allies, saying that they've often exhibited 'really bad dating practices' beyond the labels, shifting the power balance to one with which she wasn't comfortable.

'It's easy enough to put a bunch of great-sounding things in your profile ("intersectional feminist ally", "polyamorous"), but for me it often didn't become clear until much later on that these identifications and the behaviour weren't really matching up,' she says.

'Feminism and polyamory are things you have to learn, and mistakes are made, but I've definitely encountered several scenarios in which I trusted people who said they were committed to these, and yet still did things that were very much not in line with those commitments at all.'

Musician Jean Smith joined Lavalife back in 2001, when online dating was still a relatively new concept. In

2006 her band, Mecca Normal, released *The Observer*, an album based on her experiences, subtitled *A Portrait of the Artist Online Dating*. Music critic Jessica Hopper called it 'a grim, intimate picture of the solitary struggle for connection', revealing the Canadian musician's relationship with herself as a sexual being, and painting unflinchingly stark portraits of her experiences with the men she met online.[1]

'In bed he tries to put the condom on / He curses / I try to see what he's doing / but I'm pinned beneath him,' she sings in 'Attraction Is Ephemeral'. 'I hear him stretching the condom like he's making a balloon animal / he gives up and I lie there under him / two hundred and thirty pounds.'

Now in her fifties, Smith – who's also written two novels about her experiences online dating – remembers, 'I didn't want to live with anyone or meet his friends and family. I wanted to have sex and laugh more ... But after meeting over 100 men, I never did find that. I found deception and manipulation and I came to believe that it was easier for men to accomplish these things because of the distance online dating created from their social scene.

'While I didn't set out to have casual sex, I ended up having quite a few one-night stands because, after a significant amount of communication online – that included assurance that they wanted what I wanted – once we had sex, they pretty much left and didn't contact me again. Sometimes I'd see them back on the dating site in about as long as it would have taken for them to drive back home.'

Whether seeking casual sex or relationships, feminists face these roadblocks both online and offline. It's enough to scare some people off completely, and Darnell says that internet dating has certainly exacerbated a sense of disposability, or 'waiting for the next best thing', when it comes to sex – and that some online daters fail to understand that casual sex is not mutually exclusive with respect.

A woman wanting to have sex with you more than once doesn't necessarily mean she's in love with you. It means she's in love with feeling sexually satisfied and empowered.

★

But among the douchebags – and there are a lot of them, especially if you're a straight woman – there were people who were genuinely pleasant and interesting to talk to, whether or not it was sexual. Some dates turned into brief relationships, some turned into friendships, and others started and ended with a bang – literally.

Where I'd once felt somewhat restricted sexually in long-term relationships, I found that casual sex borne online gave me the anonymity to do and be anything without fear of judgement. Knowing I could walk away gave me a feeling of incredible power – it was the kind of no-holds-barred feminist sex I'd always dreamt of having.

The fantasies I'd had but been too nervous to discuss with exes were fair game with these new encounters and, though I'd previously imagined I'd never fuck on the first date, I quickly found that dates became little more than pre-sex interviews – and it made me feel invincible.

'Online dating has allowed me to explore my ideas on sex positivity and what I like sexually,' says Chloe, twenty-four. 'I have less inhibitions when I'm fucking someone I don't know. I have learnt to love my body and make it feel good even though I have always felt uncomfortable with my weight and body shape – I feel sexy and empowered when I meet someone that I connect with and have wonderful consensual sex, and I have had more of it from Tinder than from meeting people at parties.'

The majority of people I chatted to for this piece agreed that online dating has facilitated a new vetting process that wasn't so easily accessible before – and created a whole new conversation around the notion and nuances of consent. Darnell puts this down to the 'degree of anonymity' that internet dating allows users, prior to meeting up in person.

'If it's just profile pictures, I can ask what you think about fisting, and you don't know who I am, and that sort of moves into a discussion,' she says, 'whereas if I was sitting with you face to face, I might not be bold enough to ask you about fisting. So it can provide an opportunity for folks to talk about things they wouldn't normally talk about – to talk about a variety of sex practices and how embodied consent works.'

Harriet agrees: the friends-with-benefits relationships she's found through OkCupid have resulted in better sexual chemistry and cohesion. 'The conversation is often geared towards seeing if you're sexually or romantically compatible, so certain questions or topics arise that often don't in general conversation,' she says. 'When I've slept with people I have met offline, the sex itself hasn't been as good, because there's been a lot less talk about what we're both into, and also less conversation to work out if we get along in a way that is conducive to good sex.'

★

My phone screen lit up.

Matt has sent you a message.

'I love giving head. What are you doing right now?'

'Not now. But what about the weekend?'

Less than a week later, we met at a restaurant near my apartment, where we politely chatted over dinner and discovered that we both loved Radiohead. We'd agreed prior to meeting that if either of us wasn't into it, we could leave without any hard feelings.

'Do you want to come back to mine?'

'Yeah.'

Ripping clothes off. Mouths. Hands. Sighs. *In Rainbows* played in the background as we learnt how to make each other's bodies sing. I felt safe. Sexy. In control. Comfortable to tell him everything I liked, and everything I didn't like.

We continued to text for a while after that night, but never ended up seeing each other again. We'll always have those few crowded hours, though – the slices of time when nothing mattered but the here and now. The breathing, soft and shallow, hard and infinite. The stillness and the silence, content, after we came alive together as perfect strangers.

★

Josie is a twenty-three-year-old transgender woman. Her gender identity has been largely shaped by the internet – years before she came out as trans, she began exploring her female self through the virtual worlds of Second Life and IMVU by using female pronouns and avatars, while still presenting as male physically.

Polyamorous and demisexual (developing sexual attraction only to people with whom she has a deep emotional connection), Josie estimates that she's met 95 per cent of her sexual partners online, and says she probably wouldn't even have a sex life were it not for the internet.

'There's not a lot of places someone like me – a trans girl with a lot of social anxieties – can go without being invaded by people who fetishise me, and then they would be right there in my face and I couldn't escape,' she explains. 'Online, I can see a lot of people, message a lot of people, and block the offensive arseholes and never speak to them again.'

Josie openly identifies as transgender on her profiles – some prefer not to disclose this publicly – because she says she'd rather get the conversation out of the way quickly. 'I'm a woman and if they aren't okay with girls having cocks, they don't deserve any genitals,' she quips.

Sally Goldner, cofounder and executive director of Transgender Victoria, says that online dating has created a dilemma for transwomen – while the possibilities of sex and dating have opened up, so too have safety risks. Of course, such risks exist for all women, but with the astronomically high rate of assault for transgender women, it's an especially critical concern.

'Do you disclose early, and if someone doesn't want to date a transwoman, you don't waste a whole heap of time with them – or do you run the risk of ridicule, rejection or possibly worse?' she says. 'There was a situation in Victoria in the late 2000s where a transwoman didn't reveal she was trans until it got really close, and then she was assaulted. It's a balance of probabilities and unfortunately if you lose out, there's big consequences.'

Kelly, thirty-one, has shied away from online dating as a transwoman after hearing horror stories from friends. 'There's a number of transwomen that I know who have tried to put themselves out there dating-wise, just trying to find somebody that they gel with, and the amount of times that they've been stood up or just treated like a joke – a lot of them are just going, "I'm not looking for jerks, I'm just looking for somebody that I can develop a close relationship with".'

Transphobia runs rife on many online dating platforms – Oasis Active has a box that can be checked upon signing up if users 'do not wish to be matched with members who identify as transgender', and many transwomen speak of being fetishised by 'chasers'.

But fortunately the tides are turning, with increasing visibility and understanding of non-cis identities. Where apps like Tinder operate on a gender binary – you can only identify as a man or a woman seeking men or women – services like OkCupid offer much more fluidity and choice when it comes to how you identify and what you're looking for. Man, woman – but also agender, transgender, genderqueer, pangender, intersex, gender-nonconforming ... Straight, gay, lesbian, bi – but also polyamorous, sapiosexual, demisexual, asexual, hetero-flexible, pansexual ...

Darnell believes this is a great step for inclusivity and education. 'If you identify as genderqueer or genderfluid, and when you go to tick the option of how you identify it's just a dropdown of male or female, you are invisible purely by omission,' she says. 'When you are seen, when you are included, you have more agency – you have more power.'

Goldner agrees that more apps should get on board with this 'free form' way of allowing users to choose their identifications. 'If people want to disclose, then that option needs to be there,' she says. 'Of course, it needs to be a general societal attitude shift, but more flexibility in terms of the basic data would be really good.'

Alice, twenty-three, is non-binary, and says that online dating has allowed them to meet people who understand what this means, making sex a much smoother and less triggering experience. 'Sexually, you get put into a box of what people expect your gender to be – so a lot of the time with men I get read as a woman, and with women I get read as a butch woman,' they explain. 'They have assumptions about what specific genders do, so if I'm getting read as a woman I can feel a guy talking down to me.

'I only slept with a handful of people I met online, but the fact that I decided to sleep with them meant they passed the test of not being a dick.'

Twenty-eight-year-old AJ also identifies as non-binary and openly states this, as well as their feminism, on their online dating profiles. 'I get messages going, "Do you have a dick?" or "What are you exactly?" – you still get shit, but overwhelmingly it's becoming more positive,' they say.

'Online dating is a minefield at the best of times, but it's really helped me to seek out other non-binary people, or people I'd like to be with. It's not always possible or desirable to use offline dating methods to find other people that are like you – a lot of queer-orientated events are quite inaccessible for non-binary people.'

Even for cisgender queer people, online dating has opened up a new world. Ophelia says she wouldn't have had the opportunity to date women without the safeguard of these apps. 'As someone with anxiety, I can't stand the loud, flashy, crowded environment of a club, and besides gay bars and the realm of online dating, it can be difficult or dangerous to meet new people as a queer person.'

Despite all the progress that's been made, and the new opportunities for those outside of the gender and sexuality binaries, there's still a way to go – many prominent online dating services are still exclusively coded in heteronormative, binary ways. But Goldner says that societal attitudes are certainly changing, even if that change is slow. 'In the late '90s, the site gay.com had a survey of gays and lesbians that asked, "Would you date a trans person?" and 81 per cent said no. The good news is that things are shifting.'

★

As the daughter of conservative Muslim parents, twenty-eight-year-old Randa grew up with certain ideas about sex and relationships. Even now, her father doesn't want her to date at all – and her mother, while slightly less traditional, wants to background-check men before Randa can go out with them.

Randa signed up to eHarmony in 2014 in pursuit of a serious relationship, and then started using Tinder, through which she's been able to experiment sexually in a way she never thought possible. Her parents have no idea about her secret life, or that she's bisexual.

'To say that my conservative Muslim upbringing and my sexuality clash is an understatement,' she says. 'I felt broken and dirty for liking women as well as men for a very long time.'

Randa's best sexual experience was with a woman she met on RSVP. A weekend coffee date turned into another date the next day, and the day after that, and a movie night the following weekend – where they finally hooked up, and Randa had her first encounter with a woman.

'She was very experienced, but she was also patient and kind,' Randa remembers. 'She was happy to let me explore and take my time and it was my experience with her that made me realise that, yes, sex actually could be pretty amazing. She's become a really good friend of mine. We're both single at the moment so we still sleep together. The sex is always really, really good – really pleasurable and never rushed.'

Once, a man from Randa's cultural background messaged her to say she should be locked up and taught her place for openly identifying as a feminist online. As a result, she's stopped mentioning her heritage on dating sites: 'I'm not ashamed of who I am or of my family, but I don't want to marry a man from that background who has the same beliefs. I'd rather stay single.'

For women like Randa and me, online dating provides an opportunity to break free of the cultural barriers placed upon us by traditional families and backgrounds. It's a chance to write our own stories the way we want to, with taboos like sexual pleasure smashed to pieces and rebuilt as our most basic bodily rights.

'I've found it incredibly empowering,' Randa says of her online dating experiences. 'Choosing who I want to date and sleep with, and saying no to people I don't want to date or sleep with, has been wonderful. I'm getting to know my own body and my own mind and what I want.'

★

In the years since I started online dating, I've experienced things I never thought I would or could.

Through Tinder, I met a man I fell head over heels for. He ended up breaking my heart, but not before we experienced sex together in a way that I didn't know could exist – simultaneous orgasms, physical and emotional closeness, perfect synchronicity. I've never needed a man to teach me how to love my body, but being with him made me feel more sexually powerful than I ever had before, and I carry that with me everywhere I go.

I kissed people I never saw again. I fucked people I never saw again. I kissed and fucked people whom I now happily call my friends. For a time, casual sex broke me – I grew tired of ghosters, of disrespect and entitlement – but ultimately, it ended up saving me.

Struggling for so long with vaginismus, I finally learnt, through online dating and casual sex, how to let go of my fears. By playing a part with men I didn't know or care about, knowing full well that I'd never have to see them again if I didn't want to, I was able to shed the skin of the girl who was scared of sex, and perform the role of the liberated, confident woman.

After a while, I didn't need to pretend anymore.

I became her.

THE POWER OF SEXUAL PLEASURE AND
OWNERSHIP OF ONE'S SEXUAL SELF – IN
ALL ITS FACETS – CAN FREE WOMEN
FROM WHAT SOCIETY EXPECTS OF AND
ACCEPTS FROM THEM.

SEXUAL PLEASURE AND EMPOWERMENT: A BRIEF (HER)STORY

JESSAMY GLEESON

Sexual pleasure can play a key role in women's empowerment. When it comes to women's bodies, we have thousands of years of global history that detailed women's disempowerment. And although I may be guilty of recounting some of this history across this chapter, I also want to highlight the power that lies in sex, and in pleasure.

In the twenty-first century, contemporary feminism has an opportunity to expand, discuss and examine women's sexuality in a way never possible before. While a lot of us are a lot more open about 'doing it', and actively embrace our sexuality, this is not a choice available to all women. It hasn't always been this way – and women are once again pushing back against a society that slut-shames them for enjoying their sexuality. Slut-shaming itself is a relatively new term for an age-old idea: actively shaming a woman for her sexual practices or behaviours, with or without basis. The truth is, however, that the power of sexual pleasure and ownership of one's sexual self – in all its facets – can free women from what society expects of and accepts from them.

A (very) brief history of the regulation of women's sexuality

To understand the importance of sex positivity and women's attempts to (re)claim their right to be sexual, we must first recognise the long history of women's bodies and desires being regulated. The oppression of women's sexuality has featured in all cultures: as Eric Berkowitz puts it, men have 'measured their power in terms of how effectively they could suppress the rights of women'[1] – and this extended to the control and regulation of how, when and with whom women had sex. (In a historical sense, I'm referring to the 'p in the v', vaginal-penetrative style of sex. But, of course, there are many other ways of doing it.)

According to Berkowitz, one of the earliest capital punishment laws in recorded history addressed the adulterous behaviour of women.[2] The Sumerian Kingdom of Ur-Nammu (circa 2100 BC) enforced what was known as 'Law No. 7' – a law which stated that married women who seduced other men were to be killed, while their lovers were set free with no punishment. Male lovers – or rapists – of married women didn't always get off scot free, however; sometimes, they were made to pay a fine. One of the original recorded western legal systems, the Babylonian Code of Hammurabi, defined women's bodies as men's property – as laws have continued to do until almost the present day. The Babylonian law treated rape as property damage, and required the rapist to pay a fine to either the husband or father of the woman, with nothing to go to the woman herself.

Across the eighteenth dynasty of Egypt (circa 1570–1397 BC), you could find other examples of women's sexuality being unfairly controlled. Where Egyptian pharaohs of the time were allowed to take many wives (including their sisters, half-sisters and daughters), women were not afforded the same licence. A number of royal Egyptian daughters were bound to only marry their fathers, in order to keep bloodlines pure. Elsewhere, the Ancient Greeks – despite their contemporary reputation for freewheeling sex – still kept their daughters and wives behind closed doors for much of their lives. However, the reasons for isolating women were not just because they were expected to be pure and chaste. Instead, it was because women 'enjoyed sexual intercourse more intensely than men ... and that if not segregated and guarded women would be insatiably promiscuous'.[3]

This idea of women as being grounded in the lustful, physical and material was to show itself across a variety of times and locations. There have been many depictions of loose women in various artforms throughout history, but these weren't usually an outright celebration of women's sexuality – just look at the supposed witches condemned across the sixteenth and seventeenth centuries in Europe and the United States. At the time of the Salem witch trials, women were commonly described as 'the daughters of Eve', as they were seen to be more prone to temptation. A woman's purported lustfulness and frailty were used to condemn her: suspected witches were accused of selling their soul to the Devil through sex. Meanwhile, the Puritans – convinced of men's intellectual and moral superiority – presumed 'that the worship of Satan in the netherworld would be managed by women'.[4] Essentially, this meant the Puritans believed that women would be managing Satan's entire netherworld for him – an impressive promotion for women, by my standards.

Moving into the twenty-first century, it's clear that men still feel entitled to both comment on and claim women's bodies. A study that examined the behaviour of teenage boys and girls in US high schools concluded that teenage girls were far more likely to experience physically invasive forms of sexual harassment at the hands of teenage boys than the reverse.[5] These attitudes were further reflected in the research of Martin Daly and Margo Wilson, who investigated the attitudes of husbands towards their wives, and consideration of women as men's 'property'. They point out that 'men's minds readily construe love and marriage in proprietary terms' and that violating these terms can often lead to violence and danger – with the result being that male sexual entitlement constitutes the major driver of violence in a relationship, regardless of which partner is finally slain.[6] At this point, it's worthwhile noting two modern-day rights that our grandmothers and mothers were not necessarily entitled to if and when they entered into marriage. The criminalisation of rape within marriage only came about in Australia during the 1980s, and US courts refused to prosecute abusive husbands until the 1970s, with the only exception being if the husband had actually killed his spouse.

One of the clear points to emerge from the above is that some forms of sex and sexuality have been encouraged, while others have been punished. Monogamous marital sex for the purpose of reproduction typically sits at the top of the hierarchy, with other acts falling beneath it according to various cultural taboos of the time. The past is, as Thomas Dowson points out, 'always already heterosexual'.[7] To this, I would add, the past is also *historical*, in that it typically examines the narratives of men. This is confirmed by Barbara Voss and Robert Schmidt, who point out that historical records of women's sexuality outside marriage have been obscured – queer sex between women, sex as pleasure, and masturbation were all largely overlooked by archaeologists due to them viewing history through a 'lens of essentialist gender stereotypes'.[8]

Second-wavers and the sexual revolution

Across the twentieth century, a number of scientific and societal changes saw women being able to more readily lay claim to their own sexuality and pleasure. If the first wave of feminism was nominally about securing women's rights to vote, then the second wave of feminism was more broadly about acquiring rights related to women's bodily autonomy.[9] As early as the 1940s and 1950s, sexologists had begun to detect a shift in the sexual habits of women born after 1900. There was an increase in masturbation, petting and premarital intercourse, which was partly attributed to feminist campaigns against sex work: some feminists of the time encouraged men to avoid seeking out sex workers, and to look for sexual satisfaction in romantic relationships instead. The sexual revolution spread – both before and after World War II – from the dance halls and jazz clubs of inner-city areas to rural towns. In contrast, gay subcultures that had thrived over the first thirty years of the twentieth century were faced with a growing onslaught of new censorship regulations. As more people publicly identified as gay, there was a 'McCarthyist crackdown' in response to this visibility.[10]

By the 1960s and 1970s – the era of free love – people's attitudes to sex were much more liberal. One particularly significant development was the pill, which was released to the public in Australia for contraceptive use in 1961. Although the pill was initially only made available for married women, the Whitlam government lifted these restrictions in 1972, in order to ensure affordable and equitable access for all women.

One of the most well-known texts from the time, Germaine Greer's *The Female Eunuch*, encouraged women to initiate sexual advances and enjoy sex. But for feminists, the sexual revolution was not always welcomed with open arms. The problem was – and to some extent still is – that not all women are able to be sexually free. We're far from existing in a world in which all women are able to embrace their sexuality (or, at times, their lack thereof) fully without fear of censure.

After the sexual revolution of the 1960s and 1970s, western feminists reached an interesting division: that of the 'sex wars' or 'pornography wars' of the 1980s and beyond. Around this time, feminists started to speak out against the objectification of women in media, most notably in advertising. Jean Kilbourne's work highlighted how women have been sexualised in the mainstream media across a number of decades, and how women's bodies are often reduced to 'things'. This point was further expanded by Dane Archer et al., who summarised five different studies of gender difference in facial expressions and found that women's body parts were more likely to be featured than women's faces, particularly when contrasted to men. According to their research, 'men are represented by their heads and faces; women are represented using more of their bodies'.[11]

By the time we reached the 1980s, the sex wars had begun to draw sharp divides between sections of feminist thought, leading to the development of the 'pro-sex' and 'anti-sex' factions. These terms, however, don't articulate the sentiments on both sides – instead, there were deep differences related to women's sexual agency and the social forces at play, as well as cultural complexities.

Sex-positive feminism

On the one hand, traditionally 'radical' feminists argued that understandings of sex were, at the time, characterised by an ideology of sexual objectification and that sexuality in a patriarchal society was a tool of male domination. However, 'liberal' feminists argued that we should reclaim control of female sexuality and be able to choose how we seek pleasure. The radical feminist perspective was critiqued for linking women's fantasies of sexual dominance only to patriarchal values – but at the same time, the liberal account was also judged as requiring further emphasis on hidden power structures. As Breanne Fahs outlines, the discussion centred on women's *freedom to* practise their own sexuality in whatever way they personally preferred, as opposed to women seeking *freedom from* doing what patriarchal expectations required of them as women.[12] An extreme example of this spectrum is that radical feminists oppose all forms of sex work, while liberal feminists believe it can be undertaken ethically.

More simply – if the liberal feminist account of sex is that a woman consents to a night of S&M-style sex (or, for that matter, a simple nude photo sent to her partner), how do we consider her consent to be truly given, and what power structures may have influenced her? Matters of sexual consent have since advanced from the initial 1980s debate, and today we understand that sexual consent needs to be given *freely*, and in *agreement* with your partner/s. What this means among sex-positive feminists is that sexual consent is embodied, and informed: it's not just a yes, it's an *enthusiastic* yes.

A key term that emerged from this debate was sex-positive feminism, or sex positivity. Sex-positive feminism, as understood in contemporary terms, can refer to the belief that sexual freedom is closely tied to gender equality and personal freedom, and that sex has the ability to empower individuals. It is a *potentially* positive element of one's life, and it does not mean we should not question the forces that may result in negative experiences with sex and sexuality. If a person has had wholly negative experiences with sex, sex positivity might question whether they have been supplied with enough information, support, and opportunities for choice.[13]

These understandings of women's sexuality and bodily autonomy lead us to recognise some wider contemporary complications. In particular, the harm that has come from historically reducing women to bodies – particularly *sexual* bodies – becomes evident in forms of victim-blaming, and the normalisation of sexual violence – or what is often described as rape culture.

Rape culture

If you're wondering at this point what rape culture actually is, that's okay. There are a bunch of different definitions out there. One thing that a number of feminists can agree on about rape culture is that it is a complex, multi-layered set of beliefs (including jokes, images, laws, music and imagery) that perpetuates violence against women and sexual coercion – in essence, rape culture condones the physical and emotional intimidation of women for the purpose of sex.[14] It normalises the belief that women should see sex not as a pleasurable experience, but as something to be compelled into. Rape culture encourages male sexual aggression, and regards male violence towards women when in pursuit of sex or romance as 'sexy'. Just think of an example in which men are praised for their (unwanted, aggressive) pursuit and stalking of women – their actions are actively encouraged, while the woman is told that this man truly loves her and she must have invited this attention. Why else would he be following her everywhere, and sending her unsolicited texts, emails and presents?

Clearly, rape culture prevents women embracing and enjoying sex in all its forms – which is the focus of this book. Rape culture means that Jennifer Lawrence is crucified when her private photos are stolen and disseminated, while Robin Thicke can sing the biggest song of 2014 about the 'blurred lines' of consent.

But sexual empowerment can go a long way to actively countering rape culture: a woman actively enjoying sexual pleasure on her own terms becomes a radical act. It flies in the face of what we're told our sexuality *should* be, one in which we are submissive, passive and compliant.

In a recent study, Charlene Senn and her colleagues enlisted over 800 women to undertake one of two activities focusing on sexual assault and rape. The 'resistance' group attended three group sessions discussing concepts such as risk assessment and self-defence when attempting to prevent sexual assault. Following this, the same participants also attended a session discussing sexuality and relationships, which was designed to increase their awareness of their own sexual desires and relationship requirements. Meanwhile, the other group were given a series of brochures on sexual assault and rape, and were asked to read the information in the brochures.

Unsurprisingly, the results of this study demonstrated that the women who attended the sessions discussing sexuality and relationships were faster to actively identify risks related to rape and assault than their counterparts who only read the brochures.[15] From this, we can understand something quite simple: ensuring that women know what they want from relationships and from sex makes it more likely that women will claim what they want, and reject what they don't. And by saying yes to sex when we genuinely mean yes, we also highlight that a no is a genuine no – not an indication to try harder.

When women reclaim sexual pleasure, they challenge the inherent masculinity often associated with sexuality.

As Jill Filipovic points out, sex has long been understood as something that men do *to* women, instead of something that all parties do *with* each other.[16] By acknowledging women's sexuality, we also move into acknowledging that there is more than just one active, male form of sexuality. We can then view male sexuality within a wider scope – one in which women's sexuality is viewed to be equally valuable.

Of course, when we discuss 'men's' and 'women's' sexuality, it should be with the understanding that not all women – and indeed not all men – behave in this manner when it comes to their sexuality and sexual desires, and that not all people identify as either/or. However, (cis) men are disproportionately the perpetrators when it comes to sexual assaults, rapes, and the harassment and stalking of women – and the climate we exist in permits men to aggressively pursue women. While personal responsibility needs to take precedence in preventing these crimes, the wider culture also needs to change. Women can challenge the 'aggressive' forms of sexuality that they often play witness to in several ways – but ultimately their ability to do so lies within their right to make and defend other choices in their lives.

Sexuality and choice

The issue of women's sexuality is complicated because it exists within wider patriarchal constructs. Some feminists have argued that it is impossible to theorise and discuss women's sexuality while operating within a patriarchal system, and have instead proposed that these considerations need to be postponed until women are free (or freer) from male oppression. However, others view this as an unacceptable denial of women's agency in how they wish to engage with their own sexuality. This debate is summarised by Rosalind Gill:

> On one side of the argument are those who mobilise women's 'choice', 'agency', and 'empowerment' to champion aspects of 'sexualised' culture such as pornography [or] burlesque … these activities can be defended … because they are 'empowering'. On the other, empowerment is regarded merely as cynical rhetoric, wrapping sexual objectification in a shiny, feisty, postfeminist packaging that obscures the continued underlying sexism.[17]

The central question of this debate revolves around empowerment: are women who openly and actively embrace their sexuality (including those who practise burlesque or enjoy pornography) empowered, or are they simply doing what patriarchal society expects of them?

The answer, of course, comes down to the thorny concept of choice. Throughout this book are examples of women actively choosing their sexual experiences, and imparting their own unique versions of their sexuality. Some conform to dominant narratives and expectations of women's sexuality, and others don't. But the thing that brings these stories together is the power of exercising the agency in choosing sex as a form of pleasure – one that can be inherently political, but can also exist for itself.

Many contemporary feminists embrace sexual pleasure as a radical tool: studies have demonstrated that sexual pleasure can contribute to empowerment, and can undermine patriarchal controls of women.[18] By positioning women as weak, or susceptible to damage or sexual attack, we can give legitimacy to patriarchal narratives of control and protection.[19] Rather, we should encourage women to find empowerment in seeking and achieving sexual pleasure – in all its diversity. The oppressive nature of patriarchal sexual politics cannot be effectively undermined by censorship, but it can be transformed by a reimagining of sexual relations, power and desire.

To wit, I would simply state that women's sexual pleasure should be discussed *by women*. In Australia, we live in a world saturated in images of sexualised women. Advertising agencies tell us what sex should look like: lacy lingerie, flowers, melting candles – and Caucasian people no older than twenty-five. This is a very specific form of sexuality and, look, for some people it might really rock their socks. I'm in no way advocating the banning or censorship of these images (quite frankly, that can lead to larger problems related to the invisibility of women's sexuality), but I would like to see a broadening of our horizons when it comes to understanding what women's sexuality is all about. It's about pleasure with other women, with men, with gender non-conforming people, with multiple partners, or on your own. But the most important thing is that women's sexuality belongs to *women*.

FOR THE FIRST TIME IN DECADES,
MY TIME, MY BODY AND MY LIFE ARE
ENTIRELY MINE. AND I HAVE DISCOVERED,
SOMEWHAT TO MY SURPRISE,
THAT NOT ONLY DO I LIKE IT THAT WAY,
I ABSOLUTELY *LOVE* IT.

THE JOY OF NOT DOING IT

JANE GILMORE

Sex and sexuality are central to our identity. The words we use for them are not just expressing our sexual preferences; they define who we are. I am gay, I am straight, I am queer – these are descriptions of who I am, not just what I do.

Our relationships are equally defined by sex. My lover, my friend, my spouse, my fuck buddy – the sexual content of my relationships defines their level of intimacy, as if intimacy were a function of the genitals, rather than of the heart and mind. My lover is given greater intimacy status than my friend – I have sex with my lover and not my friend, so greater intimacy is assumed, despite it rarely being true. Sex so permeates our understanding of our place in the world that not identifying as a particular sexuality, or not defining a relationship in terms of its sexual content, is seen as an indication of dysfunction.

But what if the most liberating, joyous choice you made about sex was to *not* have sex? Not for a day or a month, but indefinitely.

Oooooh! The judgement!

Nothing is more open to question, evaluation and condemnation than women's bodies and the choices we make about sex.

Am I fuckable? Am I available? Willing? Eager? Too eager? If I'm not fuckable, why not? Am I too old, too fat, too damaged, too different, too fierce, too independent, too bitter – too *something*, because I'm a woman, so there has to be a reason for my unfuckability. How can men evaluate my worth without determining how fuckable I am? If I choose to remove fuckability from my identity, who am I? How do I define myself to others if they can't orient me by sex or sexuality?

The answer, I have discovered, much to my joy, is that I have become more *me* than I have ever been before.

This wasn't a snap decision: I wasn't swearing off men (as, admittedly, I have done before) after a particularly bad breakup. It was more of a slow realisation that being independent and alone is not something to fear; it's something to revel in.

My sexuality and sexual availability has been a constant presence in my life, since I was almost too young to even understand what it was. Like most women, the outside world forced it into my awareness just as I was on the cusp of puberty. I can remember being twelve and curling down on trains, trying to hide my legs behind my school bag (not an easy thing to do as I was already close to six feet tall by that time). Jokes on my thirteenth birthday from supposedly benign uncles about beating men off with a stick; cat-calling and whooping from men in cars as I was walking home from the milkbar with a pocket full of choc drops when I was fourteen. Even when I was old enough to join the game and have fun with it, sex was always part of how the world and I interacted. There were times when I loved it. There was power in being the woman who could kick arse on a pool table and do it in high heels and a '90s micro mini. So hot, so fuckable, so desirable. It felt good to have that.

Falling in love for the first time was a revelation. My first real love, when I was seventeen, was the most beautiful boy. We called him Adonis David; my friends from those days still sigh when we talk about him. I loved him the way you can only love someone at seventeen, with an all-consuming passion that swept everything else from my heart. Love so strong that even the memory of it still warms me now. With him I learnt about passionate tenderness and devotion in sex – love so strong that my body wasn't enough to contain it.

I have loved other men since him, even though, of course, I never thought I would. Love has been wonderful, enveloping, comforting, dangerous, complicated, frustrating and calm. Sex and love get tangled: I've loved men I didn't really feel great passion for, and mistaken overwhelming passion for love. And, needless to say, I've had sex where love was never going to be a factor. There's such exhilaration in being swept up in desire with a stranger; it's powerful and exciting, even more so because it's fleeting.

But after more than twenty years of all those experiences of love, sex, and love and sex, something started to change. It wasn't just about the ebb and flow of relationships with other people; it was my relationship with myself.

Part of it was to do with my children growing up. Children, when they're little, demand a great deal – not just time but also emotion and physical contact. As they grew, they slowly found other people to fulfil those needs. I know some parents feel that as a loss, and I guess I have a bit, but mostly I've watched them move away with a feeling of pride, perhaps even a slight sense of relief. They'll make the usual mistakes, but mostly they choose great people to love and be loved by, and they're safe; most of my job as a mother is done.

Around the same time that was happening, I suddenly became single again.

So, for the first time in decades, my time, my body and my life are entirely mine. And I have discovered, somewhat to my surprise, that not only do I like it that way, I absolutely *love* it.

As I write this, I'm curled up on a chair, covered in dogs and blankets; the apartment is empty and the space is mine. I can sit here all night, writing, thinking, watching TV – or just doing nothing. I don't have to negotiate my life, my choices or my body with anyone. I've never had that ownership of my own space before. I love it more than toast.

Sex is a part of and apart from that, because reclaiming my space means taking all of it away from the physical intimacy of sexual relationships. Even fleeting encounters require some level of negotiation: can I stay, will you go, will we do it again, was it good, how good, will I see you again? Closer connections require even more: have you got time for me, what can you give me, what do I offer you, when can I see you, where are you, are we close enough, is it too close, where do I fit? It can be wonderful and comforting, but it demands giving something of myself into someone else's keeping.

Choosing to keep my self for myself felt selfish at first. I felt like I didn't have the right to deny it to someone who desired it. And, because women are always asked to explain the choices they make about their bodies, it was always questioned. The implication is always that there is something wrong with choosing a life without sex, and with me for wanting such a life. People assume I must be broken in some way, and sex is a terrible loss I am stubbornly refusing to acknowledge. The possibility that I might have, in fact, *gained* something is unfathomable.

But I have!

I have gained freedom, an autonomy of body and soul I could have only found in reclaiming both for myself. My body is no longer negotiable terrain; it is mine, to do with as I choose. Rejecting all other claimants emancipates my body from the internal and external demands of fuckability and makes it territory I alone have rights to.

It is incredibly, jubilantly, freeing.

And, counterintuitively, it allows me more freedom to love and more opportunities for intimacy than I had under the contractual boundaries of sex. Good sex – by which I mean enthusiastically consensual sex – can be wonderful, passionate, gentle or fierce. It can be binding, isolating, loving or purely carnal, and all those things are a dimension of life that can be difficult to replicate in any other way. But all those negotiations of power and desire mean defining myself and the people I love in relation to sex and sexuality. Life without sex means defining those things on an entirely different basis, and the answers have been wonderfully unexpected.

Without sex as the demarcation between *eros* and *philia*, intimacy is no longer defined by who shares my body; it is defined by who shares my life and my heart. Desire still exists, but has become gentler, more fluid. Knowing that it will not reach a physical conclusion makes it less physical, more emotional and more varied. Desire is not just sexual and doesn't have to be limited to my understanding of my sexuality.

Friendship has become my greatest love and strongest desire. Friendship, which places no limits on who I can love, how I love, how many I love, is more intimate and, wonderfully, has expanded to include so many loves.

Since choosing a life without sex, I have discovered a life full of variety. I have so much more time, more energy, more emotional space free for other people. My heart is not given to one person, but to dozens; and, without sex, all I need to negotiate with them are the easy questions. Who are you? Who am I? Am I good for you? Are you good to me? Do we share something? Can we connect? I have been surprised and delighted by how often the answer to those last four questions is a resounding yes. So many new people – whom I wouldn't have known I could love if I had been distracted by sex – have appeared in my life and made it rich beyond belief.

The quiet woman who sits in the corner of my cafe is a dancer; the shy woman who hovered on the edge of my life reads everything and takes a long time to question new ideas; the man who used to be a drinking buddy is struggling with masculinity and how to find a place he can fit in comfortably, in a world that expects less of him than he has to give; the non-binary person knows things about gender and history I had no idea about; my oldest friend is struggling in new ways; another close friend has strengths I never knew of and fears I'd never seen. And so many new friends, offering time, love, hilarity, tragedy, ideas, encouragement, and they have uncovered things in me I had no idea even existed.

In some ways, this feeling is akin to that first love when I was seventeen. But instead of discovering the passion and tenderness of sex, I've discovered passion and tenderness without it. Back then, my entire world became one person; now, my world has become so many people. Tumultuous desires, whether for a night or what I thought would be forever, ruled my life for a long time. Now, for the first time, I have something else, and it feels like more. I want it to last, and giving up sex to have this seems like such a small price to pay.

I have no idea how long this will go on. It might end tomorrow; it might continue for the rest of my life. The beauty and terror of our lives is that they are always changing: people arrive and leave, circumstances shift constantly, and these things are not always within our control. But the power of a choice that was mine alone means I answer to no-one but myself in this.

And there is no greater freedom than that.

LET'S FACE IT, SEX IN ALL ITS
INCARNATIONS IS BASICALLY STUPID
AND A BIT EMBARRASSING, SO WHY NOT
TRULY SEE IT AS, AS THE OLD RHYME
GOES, RECREATION?

SH-BOOGIE BOP

CLEM BASTOW

My sexual awakening occurred at the age of nine, when my male friend E and I became obsessed with Prince's 'Cream'.

In retrospect I guess it wasn't much of a surprise, as we were in the market for a new obsession; we were starting to cool on *Ghostbusters* (despite owning vaguely screen-accurate proton packs my father had made us, using only cereal boxes, vacuum-cleaner hoses, Duplo blocks, and an ozone-layer-destroying amount of silver spray-paint), and similarly *Teenage Mutant Ninja Turtles* had run its course.

This obsession consisted mostly of doing the stupidest 'sexy' dances to the song possible. Many of them occurred at Port Melbourne beach in waist-high water (all the better to drop 'sexily' beneath the waves).

I say 'sexy' in inverted commas because, really, there was nothing especially sexy about two pre-teens dancing in a manner that suggested they were being electrocuted while also having a seizure, but that was our interpretation of the song. It was like daggering, if daggering had been invented by children who had no idea how sex actually worked.

If you haven't watched the extended music video lately, it depicts Prince – presumably – planning to fuck the roughly fifty or so women throwing themselves at the diminutive superstar at a major metropolitan train station. He then decamps to a diner where said women feed each other (surprise!) whipped cream while issuing 'suits you, sir' type moans in between ordering every cream-themed recipe on the menu; Prince can only smile at the camera. While this continues, a bunch of dejected men, who look like they got lost on the way to a Miami bass event, console themselves by popping and locking desperately outside the diner windows. Then there's some dancing: *cream, sh-boogie bop.*

In truth, I don't know if I ever *actually* saw the video; instead, we'd just leap into our trademark unco jerking whenever 'Cream' began to play on the radio. All I can truly tell you is that the experience suggested to me – since 'Cream' was so clearly a 'sexy' song – that sex should be, to awkwardly purloin the words of Dr Seuss for a discussion of burgeoning adolescent sexuality, lots of fun that is funny.

Thus, when I turned the pages of my Bells Beach Surf Classic program that same year and was confronted by a sunglasses ad that featured a couple aggressively tonguing each other, I was shocked: this ad was clearly meant to be 'sexy', and yet it seemed both boring and serious. Everything I knew was a lie! Sex and sexiness were apparently not about dancing like a dropkick to one of the stupidest songs in history, and were instead about power-Frenching someone while topless, wearing mum-jeans and wraparounds.

Something must have ticked over in my mind that day because, even though it would be another eight years before I had my first shared *sexual experience* (prior to that, a few pillows got a workout), on some level I had decided that were I ever to have sex, it would not be like that. By which I mean, not like a wraparound sunnies ad in 1991, which is probably a good belief structure to maintain in general.

Consequently, the first time I had sex was about as fun – or at least as funny – as losing one's virginity can be. (And it didn't involve wraparound sunglasses.)

It involved ribbed frangers (I learnt my lesson *fast*), strawberry-flavoured lube (I also learnt about thrush) and, the best part, the fact that at the moment of what could loosely have been described as 'climax', I thought I'd heard my parents opening the front door of the house, and so whipped my head up from the pillow only to smash my nose into a low-hanging bookshelf. As Mel Brooks once sagely said, 'Tragedy is when I cut my finger; comedy is when you fall into an open sewer and die.'

My then-boyfriend and I laughed about this all the way from Ivanhoe station to Flinders Street, even as I found myself waddling like John Wayne after a long horse ride.

Since then, I can't say I've had an uneventful sex life. There have been enough memorable moments that I once, on International Women's Day, performed a 'poem' entitled 'The Slut's Progress', in which I read out – over the course of ten minutes or so – a series of one-sentence descriptions of every man I'd ever rooted. Two of them were in the venue at the time; one later texted me, 'I'm in the downstairs bar, I couldn't cope'. That was a few years ago; were I to revive the performance now, it might go for twice as long.

That's a sly way of telling you I've had a fair amount of sex in my time – more than some, far less than others – but the important bit is that I've maintained my belief, held since 1991, that sex should be fun and funny.

Let's face it, sex in all its incarnations is basically stupid and a bit embarrassing, so why not *truly* see it as, as the old rhyme goes, recreation? When I found myself in bed, aged about twenty-nine and at that moment on the rag, with a man who had somehow managed to be sexually active for a decade without encountering a menstruating woman, I knew just what to do: I climbed aboard, and asked him, 'You like David Cronenberg movies, don't you?'

Were someone to make a *Sports Tonight*–style 'Play of the Day' montage of my sex history – soundtracked, I hope, by either 'Yakety Sax' or Winifred Atwell playing

the 'Black and White Rag' – it would involve everything from wayward pink-glittery-jelly dick sheaths, to
accidental farts, to unintentional injuries, to realising I'd
given my mother my old phone that contained a photo of
a boyfriend's erect penis wearing a Barbie doll outfit.

It's true that my dedication to trying to make sex fun
and/or funny hasn't always gone to plan: there have been
countless disappointments, uncomfortable silences, dudes
with spoof the consistency of porridge from whom and
from which I hid in the locked bathroom, and a long
and unpleasant relationship with recurrent vulvovaginal
candidiasis.

But no moment sticks out as starkly as the time, when I
lived in Los Angeles, I went on a couple of OkCupid dates
with an aspiring actor. He had stubble as sharp as ground
glass, and kept trying to 'neg' me at dinner (mostly about
the fact he thought The Beatles were better than The
Rolling Stones). Naturally, I decided to sleep with him.

After about fifteen minutes of weirdly cold, performa-
tive sex – during which he seemed to be imitating positions
and facial expressions I can only assume he saw in a porno,
or maybe a sunglasses ad from 1991 – I said to him, with
a smile, 'You take this very seriously, don't you?'

In response he shoved off me, grunted, 'Yeah, and you
laugh too much,' then rolled over and insisted on listening
to an entire playlist of Bob Dylan songs, and announcing
when I asked whether we might be able to, as it were, go
on: 'I'm listening to Bob now.'

I was so stunned by that experience that I didn't have sex for another year. Perhaps my whole sexual raison d'être had been a lie? Maybe sex wasn't fun or funny and I needed to grow up? Worse, I lived in fear that I would turn on the telly one night and see my serious date succeeding at his dreams by having secured a role on a major television series (or, worse, a movie).

A year into my self-imposed celibacy, however, a friend sent me a link. My Bob-crazy date had landed himself an acting gig: a terrible short film in which his character attempted to have anal sex with his girlfriend before being dumped by said girlfriend who had now become anal-crazy. I immediately jumped on Facebook and discovered that he had in fact moved away from Los Angeles, evidently having given up on acting – probably something to do with looking like a daggy skeleton and having the personality of a doughnut – and fled to the Midwest to direct training videos.

And I laughed so hard that I nearly had an orgasm.

CONTRIBUTORS

Van Badham is a theatre-maker and novelist, occasional broadcaster, critic and feminist. She writes columns for *The Guardian* and the *Labor Herald* and lives in Melbourne.

Clem Bastow is a cultural critic, screenwriter and award-winning journalist. Her work appears regularly in *The Age, Daily Life, The Guardian, The Saturday Paper* and *The Big Issue*. In 2015 she received a Wheeler Centre Hot Desk Fellowship to work on a comedy screenplay inspired by Aristophanes's *Lysistrata*. Her dystopian short film, *Sackcloth*, is currently in post-production, and she is developing a short experimental documentary about a *Dungeons & Dragons* player. In 2016 Clem is undertaking a Master of Screenwriting at the Victorian College of the Arts. She is currently recovering from eleven years' work as a music critic.

Rosanna Beatrice is a musician and researcher. She's currently writing a thesis about race, equality and listening, and she spends a lot of time learning about blood – go figure. Her writing has been published nationally, and you can find her on Twitter: @rosannabeatrice

Hanne Blank is a writer, historian and educator who works at the intersections of body, self and culture. She is the author of numerous books, including *Virgin: The Untouched History, Straight: The Surprisingly Short History of Heterosexuality,* and *Big Big Love: A Sex and Relationships Guide for People of Size and Those Who Love Them.* She lives in Atlanta, Georgia, USA, and online at hanneblank.com and @hanneblank on Twitter.

Jax Jacki Brown is a disability/queer rights activist, writer, performer, public speaker and the co-producer of Quippings Disability Unleashed. She holds a BA in Cultural Studies, focusing on disability and LGBTI/queer studies, providing an academic framework to inform her disability and social justice work. Jax provides guest lectures on disability and its social construction for Southern Cross University, Victoria University and the University of Melbourne, and frequently presents at conferences. Jax also runs workshops on disability and sexuality. Her written work has been published in *Junkee, Daily Life, The Feminist Observer, Writers Victoria,* ABC's *Ramp Up, Archer Magazine* and *QDA: A Queer Disability Anthology.*

Simona Castricum is a singer and drummer on Listen Records and is a tutor in architecture at the University of Melbourne – School of Design. Simona's wider practice is a holistic articulation of lived experiences of gender nonconformity through music, performance, architecture and advocacy.

Deirdre Fidge is a queer Melbourne-based writer and social worker. She writes regularly for *SBS Comedy* and ABC's *The Drum* and has been published in *Junkee* and *Archer Magazine*. Her interests include mental health, feminism, and finding funny ways to talk about Australia's depressing political climate.

Jane Gilmore is a Melbourne-based writer, editor and feminist. Her work has been published by Fairfax, SBS, ABC, *The Guardian* and *Meanjin*.

Jessamy Gleeson is a passionate young feminist who has her fingers in a lot of pies. She both works in and researches social media, feminism, online activism and gender studies. She is currently undertaking a PhD at Swinburne University of Technology in Melbourne, Australia. Her research examines how contemporary Australian feminist and women's based campaigns have used social media. Outside of her research, Jessamy also assists in organising a number of feminist campaigns and events. These include SlutWalk Melbourne, Girls On Film Festival and Cherchez la Femme.

Amy Gray is a Melbourne-based writer. She often writes about feminism, parenting, and digital and popular culture. Her work has been published by *The Age*, *The Sydney Morning Herald*, *The Guardian*, SBS and the ABC.

Michelle Law is a freelance writer based in Brisbane, Australia. She writes for magazines, journals, newspapers, film and television. She is the co-author of the comedy book *Sh*t Asian Mothers Say*, and has had her work anthologised in books like *Women of Letters* and *Destroying the Joint*. Some of the places she's written for include *The Sydney Morning Herald*, *Daily Life*, *frankie magazine* and *Griffith Review*. As a screenwriter, she has received an Australian Writer's Guild AWGIE award for her interactive media work, and had her films screened on the ABC and at film festivals locally and abroad.

Tilly Lawless is a queer Sydney sex worker, who inadvertently outed herself internationally after beginning #facesofprostitution and damaged many future career prospects. She divides her post–uni degree life pretty evenly between forcing cats to selfie with her and writing rambling Instagram posts about issues within the sex industry and her homesickness. She is passionate about horses, the way queer literature has been censored and abolishing the whorearchy. You can follow her thoughts on her Instagram @tilly_lawless or various websites.

Brigitte Lewis has a PhD on twenty-first-century Australian female identity creation and the limits of using rationality to know from the University of Melbourne. She works as a social scientist, editor, spoken-word poet and writer, combining the powers of the academy with the privilege of speaking back to power at the intersections of white, lesbian, femme, able-bodied personhood. Find her most recent work at *SBSexuality*, *LOTL*, *Archer Magazine* and *Overland*. Follow her @briglewis.

Maria Lewis is a journalist and author based in Sydney, Australia. As a pop-culture and feminist commentator her work has appeared in the *New York Post*, *The Daily Mail*, *Playboy*, *Empire Magazine*, *WHO Weekly*, *The Daily* and *Sunday Telegraph*, *The Huffington Post*, *news.com.au*, *Daily Life*, *Junkee* and more. She is the host and producer of the *Eff Yeah Film & Feminism* podcast. Her debut novel, *Who's Afraid?*, was released by Little, Brown and Hachette worldwide in 2016, with a sequel to come in January 2017. She currently works on news program *The Feed* on SBS. She can be found on Twitter @MovieMazz and at marialewis.com.au.

Emily Maguire is the author of five novels and two non-fiction books and has twice been named as a *Sydney Morning Herald* Young Novelist of the Year. Her articles and essays on sex, culture and literature have been published widely, including in *The Age*, *The Australian* and *The Monthly*. Her latest book is the novel *An Isolated Incident*. emilymaguire.com.au

Amy Middleton is founding editor of *Archer Magazine*, a UN award–winning print publication about gender, sexuality and identity. She has written and edited for a host of iconic Australian publications, including *The Guardian, Australian Geographic, The Bulletin, The Big Issue, Rolling Stone, The Lifted Brow, Junkee, Daily Life* and others. Amy also broadcasts on Melbourne's 3CR and in 2014 was named among Gay News Network's Top 25 People to Watch.

Giselle Au-Nhien Nguyen is a Melbourne-based writer and regular columnist for Fairfax's *Daily Life*, writing on topics including feminism, relationships, sex, race, mental health and pop culture. She has been featured in publications including *Rookie, i-D* and *Rolling Stone*, and spoken at the Melbourne Writers Festival and the National Young Writers' Festival. Giselle is passionate about self-publication and produces her own zines, as well as volunteering at zine shop Sticky Institute. She is currently working on her first book, about growing up as the child of Vietnamese refugee parents.

Fiona Patten is a former independent fashion designer and sex worker who was elected to the Victorian Legislative Council in December 2014. In her first year as an MP, she introduced legislation that led to exclusion zones being set up around Victorian abortion clinics, to prevent religious campaigners from harassing and assaulting women. Prior to parliamentary life, she was the CEO of the Eros Association, Australia's sex-industry group, and spent twenty-five years lobbying politicians on sex and censorship issues.

Jenna Price moved in with her beloved about six minutes after she met him in 1979, and they have been married since 1983. They have three adult children. She has been working as a journalist since 1980 and joined the University of Technology Sydney in 2008, where she teaches journalism, social media, politics and citizenship. She is also a columnist for Fairfax Media. Jenna is one of the cofounders of Destroy the Joint and has been a member of various feminist groups since she was seventeen.

Sinead Stubbins is a pop-culture critic from Melbourne who has written for *The Guardian, Pitchfork, Vulture, The AV Club, MTV, The Age, Elle, frankie magazine* and *Yen*. She is currently a staff writer at *Junkee* and likes to write about teen TV shows, films about female friendship and emotional rappers.

Adrienne Truscott is a choreographer, comedian, writer and one half of the boundary-busting cabaret act The Wau Wau Sisters. Her critically acclaimed solo show *Adrienne Truscott's Asking for It: A One-Lady Rape about Comedy*

Starring Her Pussy and Little Else! won the Panel Prize at the Edinburgh Comedy Awards, and has been updating and touring ever since. She's a Doris Duke Impact Award Artist and a contributing writer for *The Guardian*, and is currently writing a performance memoir and a series about retired entertainment primates. As an artist, she is attracted to the possibility of failure as a mandate for rigour.

Dr Anne-Frances Watson is a lecturer in Media and Communication in the Creative Industries faculty at Queensland University of Technology. Anne's research areas of interest are sex and sexuality, adolescent sexuality and sexuality education, with a particular interest in mediated sexuality and the media as a source of sexuality information.

NOTES

BRIGITTE LEWIS

1   Juliet Richters, 'Orgasm', in Steven Seidman, Nancy Fischer and Chet Meeks (eds), *Introducing the New Sexuality Studies*, Routledge Press, London, 2006, pp. 107–113.
2   Meredith L Chivers, Michael C Seto and Ray Blanchard, 'Gender and Sexual Orientation Differences in Sexual Response to Sexual Activities versus Gender of Actors in Sexual Films', *Journal of Personality and Social Psychology*, vol. 93, no. 6, December 2007, pp. 1108–1121.
3   Meredith L Chivers, Katrina N Bouchard and Amanda D Timmers, 'Straight but Not Narrow; Within-Gender Variation in the Gender-Specificity of Women's Sexual Response', *PLoS ONE*, vol. 10, no. 12, 2015.
4   Meredith L Chivers and Amanda D Timmers, 'Effects of Gender and Relationship Context in Audio Narratives on Genital and Subjective Sexual Response in Heterosexual Women and Men', *Archives of Sexual Behaviour*, vol. 41, no. 1, February 2012, pp. 185–197.

JAX JACKI BROWN

1   Liz Crow, 'Including All of Our Lives: Renewing the Social Model of Disability', in Colin Barnes and Geoff Mercer (eds), *Exploring the Divide: Illness and Disability*, The Disability Press, Leeds, 1996, pp. 55–72.

2 Eli Clare, 'Laura Hershey', blog post, 10 May 2011, viewed 28 June 2016, http://eliclare.com/poems/laura-hershey.

ROSANNA BEATRICE

1 Breanne Fahs, *Out for Blood: Essays on Menstruation and Resistance*, SUNY Press, Albany NY, 2016.
2 Bruce Cushing, 'Responses of Polar Bears to Human Menstrual Odors', *Bears: Their Biology and Management*, vol. 5, 1983, pp. 270–274.
3 Anke Hambach, Stefan Evers et al., 'The Impact of Sexual Activity on Idiopathic Headaches: An Observational Study', *Cephalagia*, vol. 33, no. 6, April 2013, pp. 384–389.
4 Breanne Fahs, 'Sex during Menstruation: Race, Sexual Identity, and Women's Accounts of Pleasure and Disgust', *Feminism & Psychology*, vol. 21, no. 2, May 2011, pp. 155–178.
5 Carolyn Yates, 'Is Period Sex the Ultimate Lesbian Sexual Indicator?', *Autostraddle*, 8 February 2016.
6 Charmaine Borg and Peter de Jong, 'Feelings of Disgust and Disgust-Induced Avoidance Weaken following Induced Sexual Arousal in Women', *PLoS ONE*, vol. 7, no. 9, 2012.

SINEAD STUBBINS

1 David C Giles and John Maltby, 'The Role of Media Figures in Adolescent Development: Relations between Autonomy, Attachment and Interest in Celebrities', *Personality and Individual Differences*, vol. 3, no. 4, March 2004, pp. 813–822.

MARIA LEWIS

1 Dictionary.com, 'meet-cute', *Dictionary.com Unabridged*, Random House, Inc., viewed 28 June 2016, http://www.dictionary.com/browse/meet-cute.

ADRIENNE TRUSCOTT

1 'The role of consciousness is choice. Consciousness of movement is performance. A performance meditation practice is the choice of the performer to exercise movement consciousness.' Deborah Hay, *Lamb at the Altar: The Story of a Dance*, Duke University Press, Durham NC, 1994, p. 3.

ANNE-FRANCES WATSON

1 Dale Kunkel, Kirstie M Farrar et al., 'Sexual Socialization Messages on Entertainment Television: Comparing Content Trends

1997–2002', *Media Psychology*, vol. 9, no. 3, 2007, pp. 595–622.

2   Jennifer A Manganello, Vani R Henderson et al., 'Adolescent Judgment of Sexual Content on Television: Implications for Future Content Analysis Research', *Journal of Sex Research*, vol. 47, no. 4, 2010, pp. 364–373.

3   David Buckingham and Sara Bragg, *Young People, Sex and the Media: The Facts of Life?*, Palgrave Macmillan, Basingstoke, 2004.

4   Western Australian Department of Health, *Talk Soon. Talk Often.: A Guide for Parents Talking to Their Kids about Sex*, WA Department of Health, Perth, 2012. Available at http://healthywa.wa.gov.au/Articles/S_T/Talk-soon-Talk-often.

GISELLE AU-NHIEN NGUYEN

1   Jessica Hopper, 'SWF, 45', *Chicago Reader*, 27 April 2006.

JESSAMY GLEESON

1   Eric Berkowitz, 'How Frightened Patriarchal Men Have Tried to Repress Women's Sexuality through History', *AlterNet*, 29 May 2012, viewed 12 May 2016, http://www.alternet.org/story/155645/how_frightened_patriarchal_men_have_tried_to_repress_women's_sexuality_through_history.

2   Eric Berkowitz, *Sex and Punishment: 4000 Years of Judging Desire*, Saqi Books, London, 2013.

3   KJ Dover, 'Classical Greek Attitudes to Sexual Behaviour', in Laura K McClure (ed.), *Sexuality and Gender in the Classical World: Readings and Sources*, Blackwell Publishers, Oxford, 2002, p. 25.

4   Julian Goodare, 'Women and the Witch-Hunt in Scotland', *Social History*, vol. 23, no. 3, October 1998, pp. 288–308; Fred Pelka, 'The "Women's Holocaust"', *Humanist*, vol. 52, no. 5, September–October 1992, pp. 5–32.

5   Jeanne Z Hand and Laura Sanchez, 'Badgering or Bantering?: Gender Differences in Experience of, and Reactions to, Sexual Harassment among US High School Students', *Gender & Society*, vol. 14, no. 6, December 2000, pp. 718–746.

6   Martin Daly and Margo Wilson, 'If I Can't Have You', *New Scientist*, vol. 190, no. 2549, 26 April 2006, p. 41.

7   Thomas A Dowson, 'Queer Theory Meets Archaeology: Disrupting Epistemological Privilege and Heteronormativity in Constructing the Past', in Noreen Giffney and Michael O'Rourke (eds), *The Ashgate Research Companion to Queer Theory*, Routledge, London, 2009, pp. 277–294.

8   Barbara L Voss and Robert A Schmidt, 'Archaeologies of Sexuality:

An Introduction', in Schmidt and Voss (eds), *Archaeologies of Sexuality*, Routledge, London, pp. 1–32.

9 These waves of feminism are largely based on activism from the western world.

10 Stephen Garton, *Histories of Sexuality: Antiquity to Sexual Revolution*, Equinox, London, 2014.

11 Jean Kilbourne, *Killing Me Softly*, documentary film, Media Education Foundation, Northampton MA, 1979; Dane Archer, Bonita Iritani et al., 'Face-ism: Five studies of Sex Differences in Facial Prominence', *Journal of Personality and Social Psychology*, vol. 45, no. 4, October 1983, pp. 725–735.

12 Breanne Fahs, 'Sex during Menstruation: Race, Sexual Identity, and Women's Accounts of Pleasure and Disgust', *Feminism & Psychology*, vol. 21, no. 2, May 2011, pp. 155–178.

13 Sarah Jill Bashein, 'Sex-Positive Feminism and Safety', *The Women's Health Activist*, vol. 41, no. 1, January–February 2016, p. 8; Carol Queen and Lynn Comella, 'The Necessary Revolution: Sex-Positive Feminism in the Post-Barnard Era', *The Communication Review*, vol. 11, no. 3, October 2008, pp. 274–291.

14 Emilie Buchwald, Pamela Fletcher and Martha Roth (eds), *Transforming a Rape Culture*, Milkweed Editions, Minneapolis, 1993; Melissa McEwan, 'Rape Culture 101', *Shakesville*, 9 October 2009, viewed 15 May 2016, http://www.shakesville.com/2009/10/rape-culture-101.html.

15 Charlene Y Senn, Misha Eliasziw et al., 'Efficacy of a Sexual Assault Resistance Program for University Women', *The New England Journal of Medicine*, vol. 372, no. 24, June 2015, pp. 2326–2335.

16 Jill Filipovic, 'Offensive Feminism: The Conservative Gender Norms That Perpetuate Rape Culture, and How Feminists can Fight Back', in Jaclyn Friedman and Jessica Valenti (eds), *Yes Means Yes!: Visions of Female Sexual Power and a World without Rape*, Seal Press, Berkeley, 2008, pp. 13–27.

17 Rosalind Gill, 'Media, Empowerment and the "Sexualization of Culture" Debates', *Sex Roles: A Journal of Research*, vol. 66, no. 11, June 2012, pp. 736–745.

18 Susie Jolly, Andrea Cornwall and Kate Hawkins (eds), *Women, Sexuality and the Political Power of Pleasure*, Zed Books, New York, 2013.

19 Bibi Bakare-Yusuf, 'Thinking With Pleasure: Danger, Sexuality, and Agency', in Jolly, Cornwall and Hawkins (eds), *Women, Sexuality and the Political Power of Pleasure*.

ACKNOWLEDGEMENTS

I am incredibly grateful for the guts and grace and good humour of the contributors – the quality of writing here is so exceptional, no amount of editing and proofing ever felt like a chore. I was fist-pumping along with your triumphs and shedding tears when you stumbled – every single one of you has given something of yourselves, and the readers of this collection are so lucky to share in your insights. This is a political project but I didn't also count on it being so beautiful and warm and hilarious. Your honesty and courage will help other women and it's already made my life better.

To all the people at UQP who've poured time and energy and love into this book, thank you, sincerely. Special thanks to Alexandra Payne, who understood exactly what this book could be even before I did, and whom I have trusted from the first moment. I wasn't wrong. Thanks also to Ian See, who edited all of us with the right amount of respect, authority and gentle encouragement. Everyone should be so lucky to have editors like this and they remind me how valuable the profession is and how often thankless and maligned. Publishing is a gloriously hopeful and bloody-minded industry and you are two of the best.

Massive thanks and love to my work-wife Jessamy Gleeson, who contributes a chapter here, and also spends a lot of time managing my affairs, producing my shows and otherwise making smart, generous and tireless contributions to the feminist community here in Melbourne. She's endlessly inspiring, and if you ever meet anyone who loves women as much as you do, you should make them your best friend and co-conspirator because it will work out great, I promise.

The production of this collection was interrupted by the arrival of a beautiful little guy called Harry Bruce Pickering. He's without doubt the absolute light of my life and I'm so thankful I could return to work with him still in my arms. To my partner, Matt, and the rest of my little family, Ezra and Archie, I can only say you're the best reason to work hard and keep organising feminists – raising boys who love strong women is a great honour to do alongside you and I love you all.

So many people gave me advice, encouragement and reassurance when developing the idea for this book. There are too many of you to name, but you know how often I call on your generosity and expertise, and I thank you so much. One person who must be singled out is my beloved Kat Muscat. She slipped away from us last year and it still doesn't feel real. She wrote a piece for this anthology but we never got to edit it together, and after much deliberation it will remain unpublished. I think the words of hers we have already are more than enough to understand her true commitment to empowering all of us, by thinking through the politics of sex and gender, and being brave. She wanted everyone to be free: in our bodies, our relationships, our love and ourselves. What a woman. This book is dedicated to her memory.

For Kat, who loved love.